Online Learning

Strategies for K-12 Teachers

Wayne Journell

ROWMAN & LITTLEFIELD EDUCATION
A division of
ROWMAN & LITTLEFIELD PUBLISHERS, INC.
Lanham • New York • Toronto • Plymouth, UK

Published by Rowman & Littlefield Education
A division of Rowman & Littlefield Publishers, Inc.
A wholly owned subsidiary of The Rowman & Littlefield Publishing Group, Inc.
4501 Forbes Boulevard, Suite 200, Lanham, Maryland 20706
www.rowman.com

10 Thornbury Road, Plymouth PL6 7PP, United Kingdom

Copyright © 2013 by Wayne Journell

All rights reserved. No part of this book may be reproduced in any form or by any electronic or mechanical means, including information storage and retrieval systems, without written permission from the publisher, except by a reviewer who may quote passages in a review.

British Library Cataloguing in Publication Information Available

Library of Congress Cataloging-in-Publication Data

Journell, Wayne.
Online learning : strategies for K-12 teachers / Wayne Journell.
p. cm.
Includes bibliographical references.
ISBN 978-1-4758-0141-5(pbk.)
1. Computer-assisted instruction. 2. Web-based instruction. I. Title.
LB1028.5.J73 2014
371.33'4--dc23
                                                                            2013021783

For Hadleigh

Contents

Acknowledgments	vii
Foreword	ix
Preface	1
Online Learning in Secondary Education: Proceeding With Caution	3
Why Secondary Teachers Should Consider Online Instruction	4
My Motivation for Writing This Book	12
Structure of the Book	13
Note	15
Introduction	17
A (Brief) History of Distance Learning in the United States	18
Online Learning in American Higher Education	20
Who Takes Online Courses in Higher Education, and How Have They Fared?	22
Where Did K–12 Online Learning Come From?	25
What We Currently Know About K–12 Online Learning	27
What Can We Learn From Research on K–12 Online Education?	31
Summary	32
Notes	32
1 Creating a Proper Infrastructure for Online Learning	35
Making the Move Online	35
How to Choose Which Courses Are Best Suited for Online Learning	36
Providing Students With Choices and Helping Ensure Their Success	37
Synchronous Versus Asynchronous Communication	39
Choosing a Learning Management System	43
Additional Infrastructure Issues Related to Online Courses	48

	Summary	51
	Notes	52
2	Course Development	53
	How to Create a Solid Course Structure	54
	Establishing Effective Instructional Design in Online Courses	57
	Summary	61
	Note	62
3	Assessing Student Learning Online	63
	How to Maximize the Power of the Internet	63
	Tips for Creating Reliable and Accessible Assessments	64
	Creating a Course Calendar for Assignments	69
	Effective Online Assessments	70
	Tips for Staying Organized While Grading	71
	Providing Feedback Online	72
	Summary	73
	Notes	73
4	Building Community in Online Courses	75
	Teacher and Student Perceptions of Social Interaction Online	76
	Strategies for Building Classroom Community	80
	Fostering Relationships between Teachers and Students	83
	Summary	86
	Note	86
5	Creating Substantive Asynchronous Discussions	89
	A Case Study of Asynchronous Communication in a K–12 Online Course	90
	Factors Leading to Unproductive Discussions	90
	Lessons Learned	99
	Summary	106
	Notes	106
6	Where Do We Go From Here?	107
	The Importance of Online Professional Development	107
	Creating Online Learning for All	110
	Addressing Technological Inequities	112
	Final Thoughts	113
	Note	114
References		115

Acknowledgments

Whenever one undertakes a major project such as writing a book, creating a comprehensive list of people to thank without omitting someone important is nearly impossible, but I will try my best. This book would not exist without the encouragement and support of Tom Koerner, publisher of Rowman & Littlefield Education. Tom saw the potential for a book early on, and he and the rest of the Rowman & Littlefield staff have been nothing but supportive at every stage of the process.

I would also like to thank several of my colleagues, especially Tina Heafner, who generously agreed to write the book foreword and gave me critical feedback along the way. I am also thankful for my colleagues at the University of North Carolina, Greensboro, who supported this diversion from my "primary" responsibilities as secondary social studies program coordinator. I would also like to acknowledge the help that I received from the students who took my graduate course "Theory and Practice in Online Education." In particular, I would like to recognize the three doctoral students, Melissa Beeson, Jerad Crave, and Miguel Gomez, who agreed to let me use screenshots of their final projects throughout the book.

Chapters 4 and 5 include portions of two previously published articles from a study I conducted on a secondary online U.S. history course. I would like to thank the editor of *Theory and Research in Social Education*, Patricia Avery; the editor of *Educational Media International*, Charalambos Vrasidas; and the Taylor & Francis publishing group for granting permission for me to use those articles in this book.

None of my professional success would be possible without the support I receive at home. I am continuously amazed by the love and encouragement I receive from my wife, Kitrina, and my parents, Allen and Brenda. I do not have the words to express how much that truly means to me.

Finally, in the process of writing this book, I experienced the joy of becoming a father. Although Hadleigh is too young to understand the content inside of these pages, she is the reason I undertook this project. If online learning is to become the future of K–12 education, I want it to be a vibrant and engaging educational experience for her.

Foreword

According to the U.S. Department of Education and the National Center for Education Statistics, the widespread use of technology in American education is evidenced by the dynamic increases in computer and Internet access, technology expenditures, and online enrollment. In 2009, 97% of K–12 teachers had one or more computers in their classrooms, creating a ratio of approximately one computer for every five students. Moreover, almost all classrooms were equipped with internet access.

In the same year, 4.6 million college students took at least one course online. Billons of educational dollars poured into technology with the hope that its innovative application would improve our schools. In 2011, approximately $2.9 billion were spent on e-learning in K–12 education, making this the fastest growing area of technology spending. In 2012, an estimated two million K–12 students took online classes. Some sources even suggest that in as little as a decade, the majority of classes will be online. The potential for online learning to become a normative educational experience is more than plausible; it is inevitable. This is one of many reasons that this book is so important.

The evolution of technology in education is a fascinating story and one in which the body of research has grown immensely. However, one area still lacks extensive scholarly exploration—online education. While research does exist touting the benefit of technology in education, online learning research has been slow to gain interest. It was not until mid-2000, over a decade after online programs began, that distance education gained traction. This resulted in a dearth of knowledge in online research.

Without foundational knowledge, the quality of online learning has gone unchecked. However, critical questions have recently been raised examining the effectiveness of online learning and associated outcomes. Educators recognize that expensive technology alone does not necessarily facilitate learning. Simply adding new technological tools or creating new learning platforms will not promote a revolutionary learning environment in which all students are successful. The quality of technology-mediated learning and how online courses are designed to promote higher levels of learning are critical considerations, especially in K–12 education. This is yet another contribution this book stands to make as it has the potential to contribute to the online learning knowledge base, one that is an essential guide for online program development.

Despite the rapid growth of online learning, training in online teaching lags behind technology adoption trends. Most distance education instructors receive little to no training prior to their first online teaching experiences. For those few who do receive training, it is long after they begin teaching online and usually occurs face to face. Rarely are teachers exposed to how to teach online through online professional development. Furthermore, most of the pioneers of online learning never engage in an online learning experience prior to teaching. This gap in experiential learning often results in inadequate online instruction and negative perceptions of online education. These trends make this book an essential resource for addressing gaps in online preparation of teachers who design and instruct online courses.

As a researcher and teacher educator for over 20 years, I have, with great interest, closely followed the expanding role of technology. My curiosity with technology led me to explore how teachers integrate technology into their instructional practices and how technology impacts student learning, especially in online environments. In my early educational experiences, I remember learning keyboarding on a typewriter and then computer programming on an Apple IIe. In college, I spent hours in the computer lab wishing I could have my own personal computer.

On employment as a high school teacher, I sought ways to integrate technology and worked to acquire the first computer lab at my school. Additionally, I remember being the only teacher who used this lab. Over 15 years ago, I had my first experience with online learning while I was in my doctoral program and enrolled in a web page design course. While I did indeed learn to write HTML code, I also found the process cumbersome and time consuming. In that same year, I took my first online course. The course was delivered asynchronously, and I still remember the isolation I felt as a completely independent learner sitting alone at my desktop computer. Ironically, I found myself ten years ago teaching my first online course in higher education.

Over the past decade, I have observed significant changes in distance education. In my own institution, we have migrated entire graduate and teacher licensure programs to 100% online delivery. Many of our face-to-face courses are taught as hybrid courses in which a varied percentage of the course occurs online. Even our 100% face-to-face courses include a flipped classroom approach in which lectures are delivered in an online format and studied prior to coming to class meetings.

The course delivery tools that we have used (e.g., Moodle, Blackboard, and WebCT) have become more sophisticated and user friendly. No longer must I spend hours designing courses in HTML code. Additionally, online communication tools have become more diverse and interactive. These include both synchronous video and audio dialogue (e.g., Centra, Wimba, Elluminate, and GoToMeeting) as well as asynchronous text and audio chats (e.g., Camtasia, Audacity, NiceNet, blogging, texting, and threaded discussions).

With each technological change, the online learning experience has evolved into a more interactive environment while simultaneously making online learning less expensive, more accessible, and comparable to face-to-face coursework. As a result, there has been a significant shift in how courses are delivered in higher education. Convenience and flexibility afforded by online learning has led to increased student demand for distance education. This along with the cost benefit of online course delivery has produced rapid and widespread growth of online learning in higher education.

Yet this phenomenon is not isolated to colleges and universities. These same technology tools have opened new learning pathways in K–12 education as well. There has been a rise of online coursework initiatives for secondary students, creation of entirely online high schools, and continued recommendations by policy agencies to promote online learning in K–12 schools. Currently all fifty states have some form of legislation regarding online learning.

My experience is more than just observing trends; it also includes an evolution in thinking that I underwent in designing and teaching online classes. Many of my early efforts were attempts to recreate what I experienced in face-to-face classes. However, I found this was not plausible when attempting to teach social studies methods online or remotely observing preservice teachers. I have grappled with how to model online effective methods of instruction and evaluate novice teaching virtually. My research revealed that online learning is not equivalent to face-to-face instruction; however, it is a comparable process but differs in curriculum and learning tools.

When these unique attributes afforded by technology are embraced, online learning can even produce outcomes which extend beyond the confines of traditional learning experiences. For example, time is not a fixed factor in learning when it occurs online as opposed to fixed meeting times for face-to face-classes. Time in online learning is a flexible asset and one that can be used to enhance achievement outcomes. The key is knowing how to effectively use instructional time and motivate learners to sustain engagement with independent tasks. Learning takes time and directed guidance from course instructors. Moreover, not every content expert will be effective in an online environment. Teaching online is a different craft from that of teaching face to face.

Over the past decade, the research surrounding online learning has also changed course. What began as an argument documenting the benefits of technology has shifted to the strategies that make technology-mediated learning effective. The evolution in course design and learning that higher education faculty have experienced have raised many questions concerning what really constitutes good online teaching. While there is a gap in the research examining online learning outcomes, especially in K–12 schools, the advantage for K–12 educators is that early lessons from higher education can be used to create maps to guide schools and teachers as they venture into the frontier of online learning.

In this book, Dr. Wayne Journell draws on secondary and first-hand research to describe processes that will support decision making by examining the purpose of online learning. He explores whether or not this mode of instruction can simultaneously address school system and student needs. He poses questions that will guide each organization in early planning and design work, allowing it to avoid pitfalls encountered in poorly developed online programs and courses. He cautions against policy decisions that rationalize online learning as no worse than traditional instruction and justify it on the basis of cost efficiency.

While certainly one significant benefit, other factors beyond financial savings must be considered in online programs. Fundamentally, Journell contends that targeted and specialized professional development is needed for teachers who engage in online course design and teaching. Moreover, the population enrolled in online courses must be a consideration in curricular planning. As Journell articulates, teaching online requires different dispositions and skills. The fact that a teacher likes or uses technology or is a content expert does not guarantee that the teacher can successfully teach online or effectively support all students in virtual learning.

Journell begins his book describing the history of distance education and online learning. He notes the reasons for its growth and highlights both the benefits and limitations of online learning. He wisely cautions that the verdict is yet undecided as to whether or not the trend toward online learning in secondary education is the right path. Specifically, he advises that online learning is not a good fit for all students.

One of the points that he makes is that online learning is often more reading intensive and demands independence in learners. Yet online courses for remediation or those used to replace a failed course are taken by students who struggle with both literacy skills and self-regulation. According to Journell, consideration of who will be taking online courses and the reason for offering such courses should guide both design and implementation. This is a fundamental factor that highly effective teachers account for when developing lessons and differentiating instruction in face-to-face classrooms. As Journell eloquently argues, "Good teaching is good teaching," no matter the delivery mode.

Online learning has the benefit of opening access to courses not traditionally available and increasing the diversity of students enrolled. Journell asserts that *anytime, anywhere* learning is foundational to an interest in as well as the success of online learning. He suggests that the benefit of increasing access to online coursework opens learning opportunities that support greater student choice, rigorous course options, and instruction targeting individual learning needs. Online learning allows for greater geographical outreach that can transcend traditional school boundaries. In addition, students have opportunities to collaborate with others from different backgrounds. The sociocultural benefits of diverse student interactions and increased academic dialogue are well supported in Journell's book.

Central to the successful implementation of online learning is the training of teachers specifically in online instruction. While Journell maintains that "good teaching is good teaching" no matter the platform, he also emphasizes that there are steps that need to be taken to help teachers with online learning and teaching differences. The 2012 U.S. Department of Education's meta-analysis of online education research acknowledges that online learning generally differs in content, pedagogy, and learning time. While a logical approach may appear to be replication of face-to-face instruction, online delivery requires some variation in both curriculum and instruction.

Likewise, Journell acknowledges that online learning is comparable, not equivalent, to face-to-face instruction. He recommends that targeted professional development in teaching online will help teachers recognize and respond to online learning and curricular differences. These experiences will help teachers develop the dispositions and skills of virtual teaching.

Factors that contribute to the complexity of online teaching and learning are described in the 2012 U.S. Department of Education's report which suggests that it is hard to determine whether positive outcomes of online learning result from how learning occurred or whether they are more a factor of what was taught or the time students invested in learning content. Other factors that demonstrate significant differences in learning are collaboration and instructors' presence in the course. As is the case with face-to-face instruction, a major determinant of student success in online courses is the role the teacher plays in student learning.

This point makes Journell's book an important resource in online learning in secondary education. Helping teachers move beyond negative perceptions of online education and perceived limitations of an online learning environment are necessary in getting teachers to recognize the unique attributes of online instruction. For example, giving students control over their social and learning interactions enhances online learning experiences. Teachers have to think differently about how to create cooperative interaction and how they will support student learning online.

Journell provides specific recommendations for how to be a successful online practitioner. For example, he takes abstract theoretical concepts such as the social constructivist theory and guides teachers in their implementation using teacher-friendly terminology. He offers many practical tips; for example, he suggests that teachers model learning behaviors for students. He also recommends that teachers share an exemplar post and create minimum threaded dialogue expectations. He provides important insights into the implications of requirements such as 250-word posts with 150-word replies, which can impact the quality and depth of student writing. He shares the importance of engaging students with the purpose of a task, an important teaching skill in face-to-face learning. He notes the significance of instructor presence in learning, such as teacher follow-up and directed interaction, as well as modeling structures that promote content analysis through inquiry. Journell presents research-based examples that model and support his ideas. This is one of many strong points of his book.

Journell effectively describes the conditions needed for positively supporting online learning among secondary students. He introduces an important dialogue that critically examines online learning and design purpose. His book is a beneficial resource for any organization, teacher, or policy maker who is seeking to venture into online education. Learning how to capitalize on the benefits of online learning requires specific and specialized planning, purposeful organization, and targeted online professional development.

Journell addresses each of these points and provides research-based recommendations for how to effectively design and successfully deliver quality online instruction. It is my hope that Journell's ideas will lead to new innovations in online courses and professional development. His book will make a significant contribution to improving online K–12 education. I look forward to the promising future of online learning as envisioned in his book.

Tina L. Heafner, PhD
University of North Carolina, Charlotte

Tina L. Heafner is an associate professor in the Department of Middle, Secondary, and K–12 Education at the University of North Carolina, Charlotte. Her administrative responsibilities include coordinating the MEd in secondary education and the minor in secondary education. Tina's teaching and research focus is on policy and curriculum issues in social studies, online teaching and learning, the impact of K–12 technology integration in social studies, and reading and vocabulary development in social studies. She has published in leading journals, such as *Journal of Technology and Teacher Education*, *Journal of Computing in Higher Education*, *Journal of Digital Learning in Teacher Education*, *Journal of Social Studies Research*, *Journal of Adolescent and Adult Literacy*, and *Theory and Research in Social Studies Education*. Her work has been recognized with awards from CUFA, SITE, and the AERA Social Studies Research SIG. She is coauthor of three content area literacy books, the most recent titled *Targeted Vocabulary Strategies for Secondary Social Studies*. She also recently coedited the book *Teacher Education Programs and Online Learning Tools: Innovations in Teacher Preparation*.

Preface

I graduated from a highly regarded teacher education program a little over a decade ago. At that time, educators were just beginning to harness the Internet's potential for transforming classroom instruction. To provide a frame of reference, Bernie Dodge, the San Diego State professor who is widely considered the creator of the now commonly used instructional strategy known as a WebQuest, first coined the term in an article published in 1995—only three years before I began my undergraduate studies (Dodge, 1995).

After graduation, I took a job as a social studies teacher in a Virginia school district which had a fairly strong academic reputation. Once in the classroom, I regularly used the instructional technology strategies that I had learned in my teacher education program. Although my instruction was hardly innovative by today's standards, I utilized technology more than most of my colleagues who had not received the same type of training, and it was not long before I had earned a reputation as my school's "technology guy."

Perhaps buoyed by that reputation, I was approached by the district's technology coordinator toward the end of that first year with a request to create an online U.S. government course for the district's new e-learning initiative. Their plan was to develop online versions of several core academic courses that students could either take over the summer to get ahead in their studies or repeat because of having failed them during the regular school year. The technology coordinator sweetened the offer by agreeing to pay me for creating the course and giving me the first opportunity to teach the course the following year.

As a financially strapped first-year teacher, I jumped at the opportunity to make a little extra money without taking time to think about whether I actually knew anything about how to create an online course. But I figured, how hard could it be? And besides, I had visions of rolling out of bed and grading assignments in my pajamas as other poor saps spent their summer vacations toiling away in unfamiliar classrooms teaching students who were equally unenthused about having to spend their days in summer school.

There was just one problem. I had never taught online or received training on how to create a virtual curriculum. My teacher education program, while placing a premium on technology, never prepared me for the possibility that I would be asked to teach online. Moreover, I had limited experience with online learning in general, having only taken one online course as part of my MEd program.

As I sat down to start creating the course, I realized that I may have gotten in over my head. The problem was not technological; the district had provided me with a Blackboard learning management system, complete with amenities such as an online gradebook, a forum for threaded discussions, and a digital dropbox for turning in assignments. Rather, the difficulty I faced was in trying to convert my classroom instruction into a digital format. Try as I might, I could not find ways to replicate the same type of interactive, student-centered learning that I used in my face-to-face classes in the online environment.

Although it represented my best effort at the time, I would be horrified to unearth a copy of that original course, given what I now know about quality online pedagogy. From a technical standpoint, I was delivering solid instruction—students received information, they applied that information to a real-life context, and then they demonstrated knowledge of the information through authentic and summative assessments. However, the course was not very student centered, and there was minimal opportunity for peer interaction.

To make matters worse, the first time I taught the course I spent most of my time troubleshooting technological issues ranging from files not opening on certain students' computers to students unable to navigate the dropbox feature of Blackboard. Several of my students "disappeared" and never completed the course despite my numerous e-mails and phone calls. Needless to say, it was a frustrating summer session for everyone involved.

I begin with that vignette because teaching that first online course was an experience I will never forget, and it is typical of what often occurs when districts force online learning into secondary education without providing teachers with the proper infrastructure and training. Although I continued to make adjustments each subsequent time I taught that course, the basic instructional format I originally created remained until I left my teaching position four years later to pursue my doctorate at the University of Illinois. I took courses there specifically on online learning theory and quickly realized just how poorly designed that U.S. government course had been.

ONLINE LEARNING IN SECONDARY EDUCATION: PROCEEDING WITH CAUTION

A decade ago, having high school students take online courses was rare. Colleges and universities had begun experimenting with online education in the mid-1990s, but other than a handful of states that had implemented generic "virtual high school" programs for a relatively small number of students, secondary online learning was still a novelty even at the turn of the century. School districts, however, are increasingly beginning to look toward online learning as a viable way of maintaining academic standards in an era of dwindling budgets and decreased funding.

As state economies have worsened over the past several years, districts are frequently being asked to do more with less. In the eyes of many, online learning has the potential to educate large numbers of students while lessening many of the financial costs associated with face-to-face instruction. Although this perception of online learning as a low-cost method of instruction is debatable, there is little doubt that this potential is a prominent factor in districts' decisions to move curricula online.

This cost-benefit line of thinking was evident even before the economic collapse of 2008. When I created that first online course back in 2003, the original intent was that the course would be used for homebound students and as an *option* for students taking summer school. However, within a couple of years, the district took away the option of taking face-to-face courses in the summer as long as the course in question had an online alternative.

Although it was never explicitly stated, it was evident that the district realized that it was cheaper to offer one online section of U.S. government than to have both an online and face-to-face option taught by two teachers. Fewer face-to-face classes also meant fewer students in the academic building, which allowed for a reduction of personnel, space, and equipment. The sum of these cuts created more money that the district could spend elsewhere.

Reducing costs, especially in this economic climate, is certainly a worthwhile goal. Where districts get into trouble is when they make the decision to move courses online without developing the necessary infrastructure required to make the learning outcomes of online instruction comparable to, or even exceed, those found in face-to-face classrooms. Fortunately, teachers wishing to create online courses do not necessarily have to start from scratch. There exists considerable research on online learning in other contexts, and teachers can learn from what has worked (or not worked) in these contexts over the past two decades.

It would be a mistake, however, for teachers to assume that simply because certain types of online instruction have proved successful in other settings, they will automatically lead to the same type of success with high school students. There are specific challenges associated with having adolescents take online courses, and unfortunately, not much research has been conducted in this area.

Little is known, for example, about the effectiveness of online courses in preparing students to take end-of-course state assessments, which is a unique characteristic of K–12 education. Also, most of the research on online education has been conducted with college students or adult learners. Adolescents often have different motivational, academic, and social needs from those typically found in older learners (Ormrod, 2008).

In other words, trying to use online learning in higher education as a model for online learning in secondary education is akin to assuming that a high school student from another country will automatically succeed when placed in an American classroom. Certainly, some elements will transfer from one context to the other—for example, a classroom in China looks similar to most American classrooms in that desks are aligned in rows and a teacher is giving directions in the front of the room—but other aspects will be decidedly different. Just as a classroom teacher should expect a foreign student to experience challenges when attempting to learn the academic culture of American schools, online instructors should expect their students to be challenged by the differences between face-to-face and virtual instruction.

WHY SECONDARY TEACHERS SHOULD CONSIDER ONLINE INSTRUCTION

Given these growing pains associated with online learning, one may start to question why teachers would even want to move toward online instruction. There are, however, a number of reasons for teachers to consider moving a considerable portion of their curriculum online. Here is a far-from-comprehensive list of advantages afforded by online instruction in K–12 education:

Online Learning Provides Freedom of Anytime, Anywhere Instruction

Online learning allows students to take courses beyond the confines of the traditional school day. This flexibility allows students to learn when it is convenient for them, which provides many practical benefits for students. These benefits are especially important for those students who often face challenges with traditional classroom instruction.

The flexible nature of online learning, for example, may actually help students stay in school. Many high school students in the United States have to make a daily choice between going to school and other personal obligations, such as caring for family members or earning money to put food on the table. Over the past 30 years, numerous studies have found that for many students, especially those from low socioeconomic status households, the need to secure steady employment is a precursor to their decision to drop out of high school (e.g., Bradley & Renzulli, 2011; Fine, 1991; McNeal, 2011; Rumberger, 1987; Stearns & Glennie, 2006).

These students are ultimately forced to drop out of school because their school and work hours conflict. Even for students who are able to attend traditional classes, many from low socioeconomic status households must work full time after school hours. These students often complain about having insufficient time and energy to devote to their schoolwork. Online education offers students in these types of situations the option of working full time while still pursuing their high school diploma.

Even for students who do not have these types of financial or family obligations, online learning can provide a way for them to retake classes they may have failed without forcing them to fall too far behind. Similarly, online learning allows students who wish to move faster than their prescribed curriculum to do so while still enjoying the freedom to work, take family vacations, and participate in extracurricular activities. As long as students have access to a stable Internet connection, they can, theoretically, take classes from anywhere in the world.

The benefits of anytime, anywhere learning also apply to teachers. By moving curricula online, teachers can manage their classes from anywhere they can access the Internet. The advent of wireless technologies and handheld computers has created an environment in which teachers may actually have greater access to their students than they typically would seeing them for only an hour or two each day.

Online Learning Has the Power to Democratize Education

It should come as no surprise to anyone who has ever spent a significant amount of time within public education that all schools are not created equal. Although states prescribe a mandated curriculum for the core academic subjects, school districts and, in many cases, individual schools decide how those classes will be structured. Course offerings often vary based on the type of course being taught and the socioeconomic status of a particular school or district.

For example, Kelly (2007) studied course offerings from public schools in North Carolina and found considerable variance in the number of "tracks" that were offered in different academic areas. Most schools offered at least three tracks for both language arts and math (lower level, honors, advanced placement), but in science and social studies, students were given only two options (lower level and either honors or advanced placement). This lack of options is compounded in lower socioeconomic status schools with fewer resources, which leads to fewer classes, larger class sizes, and students being advised poorly.

The reasons for this lack of course offerings can be attributed to a variety of factors, such as low enrollment, an insufficient number of qualified teachers, or a lack of classroom space. However, eliminating options creates situations where students are forced to take classes that are either too challenging or not quite challenging enough. Putting a course with low enrollment online could serve as a lower cost way for districts to offer a track that would be appropriate for learners who do not fit into existing options.

The same philosophy applies to elective courses. States do not mandate the offering of elective courses in high schools, so it is left to individual schools to decide which elective courses they should offer. The availability of elective courses can vary from school to school even within the same district, and, unfortunately, course offerings tend to correlate with a school's demographics.

In the school district that surrounds my university, for example, a predominantly White school located in the upper-class side of town offers its students the choice of taking either lower level, honors, or advanced placement psychology, which is a social studies elective, each semester. Yet within the same district, a predominantly African American school located in a lower socioeconomic area of town offers only a single section of general psychology per year. Given that college admissions officers often give preference to students who take elective and advanced placement courses, this type of curricular disparity is only contributing to an already uneven playing field in terms of preparing students for postsecondary education.

Research has shown that online education has the potential to narrow these types of curricular divides. For example, Blaylock and Newman (2005) studied student enrollments in 16 academic courses and 10 advanced placement exam review courses offered by the Illinois Virtual High School program. Of the 2,700 students who signed up for the advanced placement courses, over 2,000 of them came from low socioeconomic areas of Chicago.

The students who participated in the program were mostly from minority groups (60% African American, 28% Latino) and received free tuition to take the courses because their home schools did not offer a similar option. For these students, the ability to take courses online most likely improved their chances of passing the advanced placement exam and, thus, getting into college. In other words, online learning was able to level the playing field in a way that traditional schooling would not have been able to do.

Online Learning Can Minimize the Effects of the Digital Divide

Another measure of school inequity is the digital divide. If defined simply by access to technology, the digital divide appears to be narrowing. Most school report cards show that 100% of classrooms in the United States are connected to the Internet.

What that statistic does not reveal, however, is the number of computers in each classroom or the type of technology available to teachers and students (e.g., a desktop computer versus a smartboard). Research has also shown that there is a secondary digital divide defined in terms of technological proficiency that is, unfortunately, disproportionately correlated with race and socioeconomic status. Studies have shown that members of minority groups and households with lower incomes are less likely to both own computers and spend time using the Internet (Chakraborty & Bosman, 2005; Kalyanpur & Kirmani, 2005; Warschauer & Matuchniak, 2010).

If students do not have access to computers at home or at school, they will not develop the digital skills needed to succeed in the 21st century, again putting these students at a disadvantage for both college acceptance and employment. The other problem with the digital divide is that it is nearly impossible for those stuck on the wrong end of the divide to catch up (Haythornthwaite, 2007). Once low-income schools with little to no technology acquire laptops and smartboards for their students, those technologies will be obsolete at the high-income schools, which will simply move on to the next cutting-edge gadget.

Online learning offers the potential for students in all educational environments to gain equitable access to the Internet as an instructional tool and develop the 21st-century skills required for success in college and the American economy (Journell, 2007). Moreover, the same quality of online instruction can be made available to all students immediately, which minimizes the effects of secondary factors associated with the digital divide. By making quality education more accessible to a greater number of students, online learning has the potential to serve as a tool for social justice.

Online Learning Provides an Alternative to Traditional Schooling Environments

Public schooling, unfortunately, does not cater to all students. There exists a sizeable percentage of K–12 students who, for a variety of reasons, do not succeed in traditional school environments. For example, students may feel socially alienated at school due to factors associated with race, gender, socioeconomic status, physical/learning disabilities, or emotional instability.

Many students in these types of situations may respond by negatively acting out at school, which in our current educational system often results in removal from the traditional classroom environment (Gable, Bullock, & Evans, 2006; Skiba & Peterson, 2003). Although alternative schools exist specifically to educate these types of students, research suggests that the quality of alternative education often varies from district to district. Many of these alternatives have been shown to provide instruction that would be described as remedial at best (Lange & Sletten, 2002; Wasburn-Moses, 2011).

Online learning would provide opportunities for students who do not work well within the confines of traditional classrooms to engage with the same curriculum as their peers. There is also evidence to suggest that many of the discriminatory challenges students report dealing with in face-to-face classrooms—those associated with race, gender, and physical disabilities—are often minimized online (e.g., Coombs, 2005; Davidson-Shivers, Morris, & Sriwongkol, 2003; Enger, 2006). For these students, online learning would theoretically offer a learning environment that is more welcoming than a traditional face-to-face classroom, which could increase the students' chances for academic success.

Many high school students also miss a significant amount of school for more temporary reasons, such as illness or pregnancy. Often, the way in which these students stay abreast of what is going on in their classes is through work sent home by their teachers. Online learning would provide homebound students the opportunity to stay current with their studies while still providing a classroom atmosphere in which they could interact and discuss aspects of curriculum with fellow students.

Online Learning Prepares Students for College and the Workforce

A major argument for online learning in K–12 education is that it would prepare students for their postsecondary careers. According to a recent research report funded by the Sloan Consortium, over 6.1 million college students took at least one online course during the fall 2010 semester, an increase from 1.6 million in 2002 (Allen & Seaman, 2011). At many colleges and universities across the United States, entire programs and majors are being moved completely online due to diminishing resources. For current college-bound high school seniors, online learning will almost certainly be an unavoidable reality in their postsecondary education.

Even for those students who do not attend a four-year institution after graduation, it will be difficult to escape online learning. According to the National Research Center for Career and Technical Education, housed at the University of Louisville, two-year community colleges have become the fastest-growing providers of online education in the United States. The flexibility offered by online education has only increased demand for these programs (Githens, Crawford, & Sauer, 2010).

Businesses are also utilizing the Internet more than ever before to deliver professional development and other types of on-the-job training. As the American economy becomes more globalized, the Internet becomes essential to communicating with individuals across the nation and around the world.

No matter which career path one takes, success in the 21st-century American economy will most likely require that individuals use the Internet to learn a skill or engage in some form of professional development.

Online Learning Has the Potential to Promote Diversity

The "anytime, anywhere" aspect of online learning can eliminate many of the restraints found in traditional classroom instruction. For example, engaging students in projects that require them to seek diverse perspectives on historical, political, or cultural issues is fundamental to many academic disciplines. In most schools, however, ideological diversity is scarce because students matriculate from the same ideologically homogeneous local communities (Journell, 2012a).

Online learning provides the potential for teachers to create assignments in which students deviate from their local communities and interact with students in other parts of the district, state, or world. A considerable amount of research in higher education has shown Internet technologies to be effective tools in allowing students to learn from individuals with whom they would not normally interact. These cultural exchanges often lead to cultural acceptance and political tolerance, which have been defined as essential 21st-century skills (e.g., Dressman, Journell, Babcock, Weatherup, & Makhoukh, in press; Menard-Warwick, 2009; Merryfield, 2003; O'Dowd, 2003).

This same philosophy can be used in secondary education. Take, for example, an online course available to students from all high schools within that district. Depending on the size of the district, students could potentially interact with individuals from backgrounds vastly different from their own.

The district surrounding my university, for example, has 28 high schools, which run the gambit from schools with low socioeconomic status, high-minority enrollments to schools located in wealthy, predominantly White neighborhoods. One can only imagine the academic and cultural potential that would come from having students from those schools discuss issues that commonly arise in language arts and social studies classes. In a sense, online education can eliminate the effects of gerrymandered district maps and other legal measures that create ideological and socioeconomic segregation within individual school districts.

Online Learning Offers Flexible Learning Environments

Another frequent complaint from teachers is the lack of instructional time afforded by traditional classroom schedules. Especially as more high schools turn to variations of block scheduling, which research suggests actually creates less time for classroom instruction (Lewis, Dugan, Winokur, & Cobb, 2005), teachers are constantly challenged to cover curriculum in meaningful ways. These 90 minute, semester-long classes often force teachers to quickly or superficially cover material, yet they are still expected to meet the demands of state end-of-course testing.

The U.S. history curriculum in North Carolina, for example, is quite dense. The amount of time teachers can allot to major events such as the Civil War is usually only one or two 90-minute class periods in order to meet district pacing guides. As a result, instruction of these topics tends to be lecture based and often contains very little student-centered instruction. Moreover, if a student has to miss a day or two of school, it is not implausible that he or she would miss the entirety of the teacher's Civil War instruction.

Online learning provides a more flexible learning environment for students. Certainly, deadlines need to be set for students, even online. However, the flexibility of online learning does not pigeonhole subjects into 50- or 90-minute blocks of time.

Students can instead spend as much time as they need exploring the subject for themselves with the resources provided by their teacher. The anytime, anywhere aspect of online learning also affords students the opportunity to schedule their instruction around any unexpected issues that may arise that would normally force them to miss school. In other words, by moving instruction beyond classroom walls, online learning can actually create more time for students to engage with subject matter and allow them to learn at a pace that is more conducive to their individual needs.

Online Learning Meets Students' Technological Proficiency

Much has been written about the technological proficiency of the so-called millennial generation (e.g., Howe & Strauss, 2007). Skeptics are quick to point out, however, that just because a student can find videos on YouTube and post a status update on Facebook, it does not mean that the student can successfully use the Internet for academic purposes (e.g., Tally, 2007). Yet the fact remains that most of today's high school students are online more often than they are not.

A recent study of more than 800 high school students whose families were classified as "low income" found that over 90% were on the Internet on a regular basis. More importantly, these students reported feeling comfortable with basic technological processes such as printing from the Internet, e-mailing, downloading and opening attachments, and using Google to find information (Greenhow, Walker, & Kim, 2010). Simply being online does not equate to academic success in virtual environments, but these statistics should dispel any concerns that high school students cannot succeed in online education because of a lack of technical expertise.

Many teachers who venture into their first foray with online education are concerned that they will spend too much time troubleshooting technological issues. Although some technical problems are going to be unavoidable, the fact that these millennial-generation students have grown up in a world consumed with iPads and laptop computers should mitigate any concerns about students' ability to navigate the technological components of an online course. In fact, most high school students will know far more about computers than their teachers!

Online Learning Creates the Potential for Lower Cost Instruction

Yes, online learning can lower instructional costs *over time*. Converting curricula online may actually require districts to spend more money up front in terms of infrastructure and teacher training, but eventually, those costs will subside, and districts should find online learning to be cheaper in the long run. Consider, for example, courses that often have limited enrollments (advanced placement courses, certain foreign languages, electives, etc.). Without online options, districts will either have to hire qualified teachers to teach these courses at each school, which creates more costs, or not offer the courses at certain schools, which limits students' academic opportunities.

Districts have tried to solve this problem through other modes of distance education, such as videoconferencing between multiple schools. However, this type of solution is a scheduling nightmare, and inevitably one group of students (usually the one with the teacher in the room) receives preferential treatment over the others. If districts created an online option, then one teacher could teach all students within the district who wished to take that particular course. This would save districts money because one teacher is doing the same work that required multiple teachers in the past.

If districts could also move sizeable programs, such as summer school, predominantly online, it would save money in terms of personnel and resources. Districts should never completely eliminate face-to-face options unless absolutely necessary, but if half of a district's summer school offerings moved online, the district would potentially save thousands of dollars. It is important to note, however, that the savings offered by online learning should not come at the expense of eliminating teachers and creating larger class sizes online. Larger class sizes usually equate to poor learning opportunities for students, even online.

Instead, the savings from online coursework come in the form of infrastructure and nonfaculty personnel. If fewer students attend face-to-face classes, then that means fewer personnel (e.g., administrators, custodial and secretarial staff) are needed to maintain the day-to-day operations of the school. Also, districts would save money on the resources necessary to transport students to school (e.g., bus drivers, gas money) and house them throughout the day (e.g., cafeteria workers, lunches, electricity).

Saving money, however, should not be the primary reason why districts or schools choose to move classes online. Creating academic opportunities and ensuring student learning should be first and foremost in all academic decisions. As the rest of this book will hopefully illustrate, properly created online courses can provide students with an educational experience that is comparable to, and in some cases exceeds, traditional face-to-face instruction. If districts and schools venture into online education with that goal in mind, then they will be successful, and the lower costs will be an added bonus!

MY MOTIVATION FOR WRITING THIS BOOK

Before proceeding to a general description of the topics covered in subsequent chapters, I feel it is important to convey my motivation for writing this book. On one hand, I am fascinated by the possibilities afforded by online learning, and I believe that those who are not on the forefront of educational change are often left behind. Therefore, throughout my professional career, I have dabbled in online learning theory and conducted research on how teachers and adolescents respond to online instruction.

In doing so, I have found that we know relatively little about online learning in secondary education, at least compared to what we know about online instruction in higher education. For teachers wishing to develop online learning initiatives, there are few manuals describing best practices to use as a starting point. This book is designed to be both a starting guide for teachers who are being asked to create an online course for their district and a resource for seasoned online teachers who are frustrated that their online instruction has not garnered the same results as they get in their face-to-face classrooms.

I believe that I come to this book with a unique background that positions me to provide practical advice to secondary online teachers. I have had the privilege of teaching online courses at both the secondary and college levels and, therefore, draw on my own experiences in terms of making recommendations that are specific to adolescents in online environments. Finally, I have developed and taught a course designed to train preservice and practicing teachers in how to teach online, and it is one of the few of its kind in the United States. Much of what is included in this book comes from the approach that I take in that course (for a description of the course, see Journell et al., 2013).

On the other hand, I feel that I am somewhat of an unusual choice to write a book on K–12 online learning because I am not 100% sold on the idea. Like many readers of this book, I fancy myself as an effective classroom teacher, and I have difficulty believing that what I do in my face-to-face classes can be replicated online. Yet I also consider myself a realist. Online learning will make its way to secondary education whether we like it or not; therefore, it is important that teachers be equipped with knowledge of online learning theory and strategies for creating engaging online instruction for adolescent learners.

I immediately become skeptical as soon as someone tries to make the claim that technology is the silver bullet for a particular educational problem. I will be the first to admit that technology is not perfect, and I think it is a mistake for educators to expect it to be. Online learning has limitations when compared with face-to-face instruction; yet, *when implemented correctly*, online learning can be highly comparable to what students would find in a traditional classroom. A well-constructed and well-implemented online course actually offers students many advantages that they would not typically find in their face-to-face courses.

STRUCTURE OF THE BOOK

The overriding theme of this book is that "good teaching is good teaching," regardless of the medium. Many of the strategies included in this book use the same basic tenets of quality classroom instruction; they just appear differently online. The subsequent chapters will serve as a guide to better understanding what successful online programs look like and how they can be implemented for adolescent learners.

In the Introduction, I provide a brief history of online learning in the United States. With online learning, just like any other educational innovation, context is essential to understanding its implications. Online learning did not infiltrate secondary education overnight; it is merely the next step in an evolution that has roots in the 19th century. I believe it is important for secondary educators to understand where online learning has been and what we have learned from previous iterations because that history is what will inform us about best practices for the future.

In Chapter 1, I discuss the different tools that online teachers have at their disposal and how each can contribute to an engaging learning experience for students. This chapter also focuses on the differences between online and face-to-face instruction and how teachers must alter their instructional practices accordingly. Creating a solid infrastructure is the first step in ensuring quality and effective instruction online.

Chapters 2 and 3 are meant to serve as a practical guide for teachers who are developing online courses and assessments. In these chapters, I discuss how the day-to-day activities of a face-to-face class can effectively be replicated online. Teachers versed in learning theories will recognize the similarities between online and face-to-face teaching. Again, good teaching is good teaching.

All elements of traditional classroom instruction—units, lessons, content dissemination, activities, assessments, group work—can work online. Each will appear differently online, however, and many require a different skill set than what teachers typically use to create these types of instructional practices in the classroom. These chapters offer teachers step-by-step directions for using technology to create engaging online instructional activities as well as tips for how to efficiently collect, grade, and provide feedback on student work.

Chapter 4 addresses one of the more challenging aspects of online instruction, which is creating and sustaining a feeling of community among students and between students and their teachers. Using data from my own research, I discuss the importance of educating both students and teachers about the need for interaction and discussion in online courses. The only way online learning can achieve the same type of learner-centered, constructivist instruction that is expected from high-quality face-to-face classes is if teachers make a concerted effort to include opportunities for student communication, both informal and academic, in their courses.

Chapter 5 builds on this idea of increased communication in online learning by focusing specifically on asynchronous discussion (e.g., threaded discussion boards), which is the most common communication method found in K–12 online education. Asynchronous communication holds considerable potential for academic interactions among students, but only if teachers provide students with clear expectations for discussion and model appropriate communication themselves. I discuss the pitfalls of unregulated asynchronous communication among adolescents and offer strategies for teachers wishing to foster engaged discussions of content in their courses.

In the final chapter, I discuss the current state of secondary online learning and possibilities for the future. There is much we do not know about how to ensure that these online courses remain both a viable alternative to face-to-face instruction and accessible to all types of learners. Specifically, the growth of secondary online learning has led to a need for increased training, both for practicing and preservice teachers, in online pedagogy. Also, there is much we do not know about how to effectively adapt online courses for students with disabilities, English language learners, and other students who may enter their online courses with unique learning needs.

As readers navigate this book, it is important to remember that secondary online learning is in its infancy and that anytime one interacts with technology, the only certainty is that it will continually change. As technology continues to improve and become more affordable, more districts will begin to incorporate online learning opportunities for students. It is my hope that this book provides readers with a practical guide for understanding secondary online instruction and contributes to the process of creating vibrant educational opportunities for adolescents in the 21st century.

NOTE

Many of the ideas discussed in this preface were originally presented in my 2012 article "Walk, Don't Run—to Online Learning," in *Phi Delta Kappan*, *93*(7), pages 46–50.

Introduction

In order to place online learning into a proper context, it is important for teachers to have an understanding of how online learning has made its way into K–12 public education. Practitioners too often view new directives as coming down from "on high" without any forewarning or explanations, thus making them less open to change. Often, however, educational innovations are not really *that* new or outside the box, and once teachers can establish that level of understanding, they are much more likely to give new ideas a chance.

This is the case with online learning. Online learning is just the latest in a long line of innovations designed to make education cheaper and more accessible. Once access to the Internet became more affordable, it was never a question of whether it would become a tool for disseminating education to students; it was just a matter of when. The fact that it took this long for online education to make a substantive contribution to K–12 education is perhaps the only surprise.

The purpose of this chapter is to provide readers with a historical context for K–12 online learning. What follows is not intended to be an all-encompassing review of the entirety of online education literature; rather, this chapter provides readers with basic background knowledge about online learning. Specifically, it is important for teachers to know

- the origins of online learning;
- the impact of online learning on higher education;
- who, historically, has taken higher education courses online and how they have fared;
- the origins of K–12 online learning; and
- the current state of K–12 online learning.

Again, this chapter is designed to be a very brief discussion of the more theoretical aspects of online learning. Readers who are interested in learning more about these topics are encouraged to consult the more comprehensive reviews cited in this chapter.[1]

A (BRIEF) HISTORY OF DISTANCE LEARNING IN THE UNITED STATES[2]

Online Learning as an Incarnation of Distance Education

Technically, the origins of online learning must start with the development of the Internet in the early 1970s and the advent of commercial Internet providers in subsequent decades. The ideological context from which online learning is derived, however, can be traced back much further. As Larreamendy-Joerns and Leinhardt (2006) argue, online education is just the latest iteration of the concept of distance learning that has been present in the American educational system since the late 19th century.

These early distance education programs were designed to make public education more accessible to those who lived far from educational institutions or who did not socially or legally have access to education (e.g., women). The earliest of these programs, the Tricknor's Society to Encourage Studies at Home, was founded in 1873. This program could best be classified as a correspondence course in which students received curricula through the mail that they then completed and mailed back for assessment purposes.

Soon thereafter, in 1881, Chautauqua Correspondence College was founded in New York and was authorized to confer degrees to students who had taken courses entirely via the U.S. Postal Service. The distance education movement only truly gained serious traction, however, after the establishment of the Extension Division at the University of Chicago in 1892. This program was the first formal attempt at distance education from a highly respected university in the United States.

By the early 1900s, many prominent universities were regularly offering correspondence options to students who could not attend on-campus classes. It is worth noting that many of these early correspondence courses faced criticism similar to that which is often attributed to online learning today. Instructors of distance education programs complained that managing student correspondence consumed too much time, and both students and instructors complained that learning was being conducted in isolation without any opportunities to interact with peers.

Perhaps most importantly, these correspondence courses faced considerable skepticism regarding the quality of the instruction that students received. Even in the early part of the previous century, face-to-face classroom instruction was considered the gold standard for public education. The legitimacy of any programs that deviated from that model was immediately questioned.

Education, just like most aspects of American society, operates on the economic principles of supply and demand. Therefore, despite the objections of traditionalists, more institutions began offering distance education programs throughout the 20th century. As new technologies, such as radio and television, gained prominence, they were soon being used as tools for disseminating curricula to students.

The Influence of the "Open University" Concept

The milestone that was arguably the most influential to the success of distance education in the United States occurred in Europe in 1969. In that year, Britain established the Open University, a major research institution designed solely for distance education. Still in operation today, the Open University "has been described as one of the most successful cases of policy implementation in the educational field" (Moore, 2003, p. 15). The university has an annual enrollment of over 100,000 students and is consistently ranked as one of the most prestigious universities in Britain in both research and teaching.

Yet the Open University maintains this level of academic quality at a per-student cost that is substantially less than traditional universities. Not surprisingly, the success of the Open University prompted other nations throughout the world to create similar types of universities throughout the next two decades. These universities relied heavily on teleconferencing, audio conferencing, and other types of instruction that harked back to the days of correspondence courses.

Interestingly, the United States was one of the few industrialized nations not to develop a type of national, "open" university program. Instead, smaller institutions, such as the Nova University of Advanced Technology (now Nova Southeastern University) and Empire State College, were created by states and based on the Open University model. Over time, established American universities began developing external degree programs to meet the demands of distance education.

As one can see, the mindset for online distance education in the United States was already in place by the time the World Wide Web as we know it today was developed in the early 1990s. It did not take long for institutions of higher education to use the Internet to continue this system of educating large numbers of students in a low-cost fashion. It is on the successes and failures of online learning in American colleges and universities that we have based much of our current understanding of K–12 online education.

ONLINE LEARNING IN AMERICAN HIGHER EDUCATION

History of American Online Higher Education

It is hard to believe that the World Wide Web has existed for only two decades, but it was in 1993 when Mosaic, generally considered the first web browser with a graphical interface, was released to the public (Moore, 2003).[3] It is amazing how far we have come in such a short amount of time. Part of the reason for this evolution is the rapid rate by which Americans gained access to the Internet, which was faster than any previous form of technological communication (Bates, 2000). According to Moore (2003), only 9% of Americans had access to the Internet in 1995, but by 2002, that number had jumped to 66%, which equated to 137 million people.

Within the next two decades, the demand for online learning in American higher education skyrocketed. Today, almost every college and university in the United States offers courses online, and many are increasingly converting entire programs to an online format. These online courses are not only being taken by students who live away from campus; many universities offer online courses as part of "on-campus" degree programs as a way to provide flexibility to students and lower administrative costs associated with teaching.

According to a recent study of American colleges and universities, online courses constituted 31.3% of total higher education enrollment as of the fall 2010 semester. That same report found that online enrollment has grown at an average rate of 18.55% as opposed to an average of 2.13% growth for total student enrollment. It is not surprising, then, that the same study found that over 60% of public higher education institutions reported online education to be critical to the long-term success of their institutions (Allen & Seaman, 2011).

Public colleges and universities are not the only institutions, however, that have embraced online education. It did not take long for entrepreneurs to discover that education was, like most enterprises in the dot-com era, a market waiting to be revolutionized by the Internet. Many for-profit, virtual universities, such as the University of Phoenix, began to emerge as a way for individuals to earn degrees from the comfort of their own homes.

Like the Open University in Britain, these virtual universities claim to seek democratization of higher education by offering courses online to people who cannot attend classes at universities. Unlike the British system, however, most of these virtual universities employ part-time faculty who often do not engage in academic research as part of their positions (Moore, 2003). The "for-profit" aspect of these institutions has caused some critics to question the legitimacy of the degrees these institutions confer, which has impacted the overall perception of online instruction in the United States.

The Perception of Online Higher Education in the United States

Given that online learning has become a fixture in American higher education, the obvious question to ask is whether the online phenomenon has affected student learning for the better. The answer tends to vary depending on who is being asked, which most likely speaks to the disparity in the quality of online courses and programs that currently exist. Returning to the previously mentioned study by Allen and Seaman (2011), their survey of university leaders found that two thirds felt online courses were "just as good" as or better than face-to-face courses, but only slightly over 10% cited online learning as "somewhat superior" or "superior" to traditional instruction.

Of course, these figures also mean that approximately a third of respondents believed online education to be either "somewhat inferior" or "inferior" to face-to-face instruction. When asked to hypothesize about student satisfaction with online courses, the majority of these same university leaders felt that it was "about the same" as face-to-face courses. Of those who felt there was a difference in students' perceptions of online and face-to-face courses, a slightly higher percentage believed face-to-face instruction was either "somewhat superior" or "superior" to online instruction.

Yet when asked about the flexibility afforded to students' schedules, online learning was overwhelmingly viewed as superior to face-to-face instruction. Overall, the only measure in which online learning did not fare at least "about the same" as traditional instruction was when respondents were asked about the quality of student-to-student interactions (Allen & Seaman, 2011). These statistics represent only a snapshot from one study of university leaders' perceptions of online education; however, they are fairly consistent with cases from the larger body of research about online learning (e.g., Haythornthwaite & Kazmer, 2004; Tallent-Runnels et al., 2006).

The one constant in all studies of online learning is that students and teachers love the flexibility afforded by online education. Most studies also report that the content found in online courses is comparable to that which students would receive in a face-to-face setting. Yet students and teachers often complain about the diminished social component of online instruction, which can lead to academic challenges if not addressed by the instructor.

Another perception of online higher education, however, is less positive and emanates from the same question of legitimacy that plagued the correspondence courses of the early 20th century. In particular, the for-profit programs that emerged in the 1990s have generated considerable skepticism from members of academia. Critics, such as David Noble (2001) and others, have labeled these types of programs as "digital diploma mills" and accused them of handing out degrees based simply on the number of tuition checks received as opposed to rigorous academic work.

A discussion of whether these for-profit programs are actually diploma mills is beyond the scope of this book. Yet this perception of online learning, although diminishing, still is very prominent in certain academic circles. As someone who has sat on several university search committees, for example, I can attest that if an applicant stated that he or she had earned an advanced degree from a for-profit institution such as the University of Phoenix, there is no way he or she would receive an invitation for an interview (at least in my department).

It is also no secret that some people will consider an academic degree that was earned entirely or primarily online as a "lesser" degree than one from a traditional program, even when both degrees come from a respected, accredited university. Perceptions, unfortunately, are difficult to change. As long as the perception exists that online courses are less rigorous than face-to-face courses, it will hold negative implications for all types of online instruction, including K–12 online learning.

WHO TAKES ONLINE COURSES IN HIGHER EDUCATION, AND HOW HAVE THEY FARED?

Given that research on K–12 online learning remains in its infancy, much of what we currently know about teaching and learning online comes from research on adult learners and students in higher education. As the figures reported in the previous section can attest, there is no shortage of online learners in our colleges and universities. From a purely academic standpoint, the literature is inconclusive about whether online or traditional instruction is more effective for student learning. Most studies that have sought to compare the two modes of instruction have found negligible differences, at least in terms of student performance on assessments (Bernard et al., 2004; Tallent-Runnels et al., 2006).

What Works/Doesn't Work in Online Higher Education

Not all online courses are created equally. As with face-to-face instruction, students are going to learn more from a quality online course than a poorly designed or ineffectively implemented one. When students are asked about their online experiences, for example, they often express satisfaction with courses that allow them to interact with others and apply material that they are learning to real-life contexts. Similarly, they express displeasure at courses that simply involve reading articles and writing papers while receiving little feedback from the instructor or their classmates.

If one were to remove the word "online" from the previous paragraph, these positive and negative instructional aspects would be the same as those typically found on teacher evaluations in traditional classroom settings. The research on online higher education, therefore, supports one of the fundamental themes of this book: that good teaching is good teaching, regardless of the medium being used. Yet research suggests that what is needed to position learners to engage in quality learning online may be different (or at least look different) from what is needed in a face-to-face setting.

If, for example, one adopts a Vygotskian (1978) perspective toward learning in which instruction is most effective when learners construct knowledge by having their existing views challenged and reformed through interactions with others, then online learning often falls short of an ideal learning environment. Research has found that there is, generally, less in-depth student-to-student interaction in online courses than in typical face-to-face courses (e.g., Berge, 2002; Kanuka & Anderson, 1998; Thomas, 2002). Although scholars are still unsure why students are sometimes less willing to interact online, research suggests instructors can take the following steps to encourage student participation:

- Encourage a positive course climate where students are familiar with each other and feel comfortable communicating (e.g., Garrison & Anderson, 2003; Haythornthwaite & Bregman, 2004; Tu & McIsaac, 2002);
- Increase instructor presence in the course (e.g., Blignaut & Trollip, 2003; Journell, 2008; McIsaac, Blocher, Mahes, & Vrasidas, 1999); and
- Offer students multiple options for interaction (e.g., Im & Lee, 2004; Levin, He, & Robbins, 2006; Mabrito, 2006).

Interestingly, research has shown that the level of interaction students have with their peers in online courses does not necessarily affect their academic performance (e.g., Davies & Graff, 2005; Herring & Clevenger-Schmertzing, 2007). Yet when courses do not provide students with a proper infrastructure for interaction, research has shown that it can have disastrous results. When students do not have the opportunity to interact with their peers and their instructors, many students become disengaged and eventually drop out of their courses.

The number of students who have reported dropping out of online courses has been found to be higher than the number who remove themselves from face-to-face classes (Jun, 2005). When asked why they dropped out, students often state that they felt as if they were learning in isolation and, as a result, it became easy for them to disengage from the curriculum. Even students who do not drop online courses often struggle due to the isolated environment provided by a poorly designed course. Instructors often report students "disappearing," meaning that they remain on the roll but simply decide to stop doing work.

Who Succeeds/Doesn't Succeed in Online Higher Education?

The literature also suggests that students who perform well in online courses may have certain personality traits that lend themselves to success in an autonomous learning environment. Perhaps the most important characteristic identified by the literature is a student's intrinsic motivation, specifically a student's ability to work independently without teacher oversight (e.g., Battalio, 2009; DeTure, 2004; Kickul & Kickul, 2006; Roblyer, 1999; Whipp & Chiarelli, 2004). Research also suggests older students tend to be more intrinsically motivated and, thus, perform better in online courses than their younger peers, a finding that has considerable implications for K–12 online learning (Hoskins & van Hooff, 2005).

In addition to student motivation, the literature cites other personality traits that correlate with students' success online. Many of these traits, such as good study habits, organization, willingness to exhibit effort on academics, and experience with technology, are not surprising (e.g., Bernard, Brauer, Abrami, & Surkes, 2004; Lim, 2001; Maki & Maki, 2002; Waschull, 2005). Other than perhaps the technology component, these same attributes would be used to describe most successful students, regardless of the type of classroom environment.

In terms of the types of students who take online courses in higher education, research has found that enrollments are similar to that of most traditional classes (Tallent-Runnels et al., 2006). In theory, online learning should remove many of the differences that exist in traditional classroom environments related to demographic characteristics, such as race, gender, and socioeconomic status, considering that online learning provides students with more anonymity than face-to-face classes. The research on this aspect of online instruction, however, is mixed.

Studies have shown that gender differences, for example, are often diminished in online courses and that females tend to develop stronger feelings of classroom community online than do their male peers (e.g., Davidson-Shivers et al., 2003; Rovai, 2001, 2002; Wang, Sierra, & Folger, 2003). In studies focusing on race, however, the research shows that members of minority groups tend to feel less comfortable in online environments. Yet the reasons for this disparity are often not clear (e.g., Rovai & Gallien, 2005; Rovai & Wighting, 2005).

Another aspect of teaching for diversity in online higher education that has implications for K–12 online learning is identifying best practices for adapting online coursework for learners with special needs and English language learners (ELLs). This area, however, is severely underresearched within the online higher education literature (Coryell & Chlup, 2007; Keeler & Horney, 2007). Given the student populations at most colleges and universities, it is perhaps not surprising that this aspect of online instruction has not received more attention.

A few scholars have suggested that online learning has the potential to increase academic achievement among students in these groups (e.g., Coombs, 2005; Warschauer, 1998). Few studies, however, have been conducted to support those theories. Given that accommodating students with diverse learning needs is an essential aspect of K–12 education in the 21st century, this lack of knowledge presents considerable uncertainty for the success of online learning at the secondary level.

WHERE DID K–12 ONLINE LEARNING COME FROM?

Given the relative success of online learning in higher education, it is no surprise that K–12 education soon followed suit. Unlike higher education, however, online K–12 education is primarily a North American phenomenon (Barbour, 2009).[4] The first attempts at creating online K–12 schooling actually occurred in Canada before moving to the United States.

In Canada, district initiatives in Alberta and Newfoundland in 1995 and 1996, respectively, called for web-based programs as a means to reach students who lived in remote areas of the provinces. Over the next ten years, the programs grew to over 20 virtual schools in Alberta catering to approximately 7,000 full- and part-time students and over 90 schools in Newfoundland offering courses to nearly 1,500 students. The success of these programs prompted other Canadian provinces to create similar programs, most of which remain active today (Barbour & Reeves, 2009).

K–12 Online Learning in the United States

Although a few small attempts at creating online K–12 schooling in the United States occurred in the early 1990s (Barbour, 2010), the first real breakthroughs came later in the decade with the creation of the Virtual High School (VHS) and the Florida Virtual School (FLVS). The VHS was started by the Concord Consortium, a nonprofit educational research and development organization, in partnership with Hudson Public Schools in Massachusetts. Bob Tinker, president of the Concord Consortium, received a $7.4 million federal grant for the project, which started in the 1997–1998 school year.

That year, the VHS offered 28 online course offerings to a group of 28 schools that paid for membership to the VHS. In terms of enrollment, the VHS was an immediate success; in less than five years, the number of participating schools had increased to over 200 and were located in 26 states and 11 countries (Pape, Adams, & Ribeiro, 2005; Zucker & Kozma, 2003). Today, the VHS includes over 600 member schools in over 30 states and over

30 countries with a total enrollment of over 16,000 students. According to their website, the costs associated with joining the VHS vary based on the type of package a school selects (VHS Collaborative, 2012).

The FLVS also launched in 1997, thanks to a $200,000 grant from the state of Florida. Unlike the VHS, the FLVS was designed to be funded by the state legislature, just like any other public school district in Florida, and offered free to in-state residents. In its initial year, the FLVS enrolled only 157 students; however, just as with VHS, the demand for online education skyrocketed in subsequent years.

By 2004, the FLVS had an enrollment of 18,000 students in over 70 online courses, and that number is representative of having to cap enrollment in each year of FLVS's existence due to state budget constraints. Although the FLVS remains free for students, the Florida legislature passed a law in 2003 stating that funding for FLVS would be tied to student performance (Friend & Johnston, 2005). Today, the FLVS has implemented a global initiative that expands its services to the other 49 states and 57 countries and provides instruction to over 122,000 students (Florida Virtual School, 2012).

The FLVS was the start of a larger movement by states to create statewide virtual K–12 schools that would be available to in-state residents. A recent study of K–12 online learning reported that 40 states have some type of statewide virtual schooling program that accounted for over 536,000 course enrollments during the 2010–2011 school year. Yet the quality and availability of these virtual schools varies considerably; those that receive considerable funding from state legislatures, such as in Florida, North Carolina, and Michigan, enroll large numbers of students, but virtual high schools in other states are in decline due to budget cuts prompted by recent economic challenges (Watson, Murin, Vashaw, Gemin, & Rapp, 2011).

Despite the decline in statewide virtual high schools, online learning is increasing in K–12 education. Statewide programs constitute only a portion of online K–12 education in the United States. Other options include the following (Cavanaugh, Barbour, & Clark, 2009; Rice, 2006):

- *Consortium or regionally based virtual schools*—similar to the VHS discussed earlier
- *Private virtual schools*—private schools that operate the same way that traditional private schools operate in that students have to be admitted and pay tuition
- *Single-district virtual schools*—full-fledged virtual schools that are offered by districts as an alternative to traditional classroom environments for students in those districts
- *Multidistrict virtual schools*—virtual schools that are operated within school districts but enroll students from other school districts within the state

- *Virtual charter schools*—virtual schools that are chartered within a district but can enroll students throughout the state
- *District-level supplemental courses and programs*—online courses or programs that are created and run by individual school districts

According to recent research, the district-level supplemental courses and programs—those which are created, run, and assessed by individual school districts—are the fastest growing mode of K–12 education in the United States (Watson et al., 2011). In a study of school districts during the 2007–2008 school year, Picciano and Seaman (2009) found that three quarters were offering online or blended courses within the district.

Overall, Picciano and Seaman (2009) estimate that over one million K–12 students took online courses during the 2007–2008 school year, and that number has most likely risen since then. The vast majority of these students are in high school, although some districts appear to be offering online options to elementary and middle-grades students as well. The fact that over a million K–12 students are taking online courses is staggering, and that we know very little about best practices when it comes to the teaching and learning that occurs in these courses is a cause for alarm.

WHAT WE CURRENTLY KNOW ABOUT K–12 ONLINE LEARNING

Online education is close to becoming ubiquitous in K–12 public education. More states are not just offering online courses, they are *requiring* them. In 2006, the state of Michigan became the first to require that *all* students take at least one online course before graduating high school.

The rationale behind that decision was that online technologies would be so ingrained in 21st-century American society that policy makers felt students would not be prepared to enter higher education or the workforce if they did not have at least some experience with online learning (Michigan Merit Curriculum, 2006). As of this writing, similar mandates have since been enacted in New Mexico (2007), Alabama (2008), and Idaho (2011). It is probably safe to assume that this number will rise as technology continues to improve and becomes more affordable.

Sadly, research on K–12 online education has not kept up with its growth. Reviews of the online K–12 literature have found that publications tend to fall into one of the following categories (Barbour & Reeves, 2009; Cavanaugh et al., 2009; Rice, 2006):

- Narratives of virtual school teachers' and administrators' personal experiences

- Arguments for the theoretical pedagogical benefits of K–12 online learning
- Challenges related to the implementation and success of K–12 online learning
- Research that compares online learning to face-to-face learning
- Research that examines issues related to students' retention in online schooling
- Research that examines students' perceptions of online learning
- Research that examines teachers' perceptions of online learning
- Research that examines the characteristics of quality online instruction

On the surface, this list may seem fairly comprehensive, but unfortunately, the literature is not evenly distributed within these categories. Considerably more has been written about individuals' personal experiences and the theoretical benefits and challenges of K–12 online learning than empirical research on the teaching and learning that is actually occurring in online courses (Barbour, 2010). Although theoretical arguments and personal narratives are useful for making the case for or against the creation of online learning programs, they do little to improve the practices of teachers and students in existing online programs.

Comparisons Between Online and Face-to-Face Learning

Based on the limited research that has been conducted, however, we can highlight certain areas of strength and concern. Most studies of student success in online classes have mirrored what scholars have found in higher education and in K–12 education broadly. For example, in a recent study of an online high school biology course, Liu and Cavanaugh (2011) found that the more time students spent engaged with course materials, the better they did in the course overall. They also found that students who were identified as participating in free or reduced-cost lunch programs performed worse than other students. Neither of these findings strays too far from what we already know from research in other contexts.

As in higher education, many scholars have attempted to compare student learning in online and face-to-face classes. Overall, the research suggests that online and traditional K–12 education are comparable in terms of learning outcomes. Much of this research, however, is questionable because of limitations associated with these types of studies.

For example, comparing quality face-to-face and online instruction when there is limited knowledge about best practices in online education creates a potentially unequal comparison. Also, conclusions drawn from studies of K–12 online learning can be skewed due to the fact that many students drop out of these classes before data can be collected, leaving researchers with data primarily from highly motivated, high-achieving students (Barbour, 2010). This concern is amplified when one considers that another primary finding of K–12 online learning is that student motivation and other personality traits are often determining factors in students' success online.

Who Succeeds in K–12 Online Education?

As with students in higher education, the ideal online K–12 student is highly motivated, organized, self-disciplined, and comfortable with technology (e.g., Roblyer, Davis, Mills, Marshall, & Pape, 2008; Roblyer & Marshall, 2002; Weiner, 2003). Unfortunately, however, the number of students in K–12 education is considerably higher than that in higher education, making it highly unlikely that only motivated students will take online courses (Barbour, 2009). As districts increase online learning requirements while simultaneously decreasing face-to-face options for students, it is reasonable to expect that many academically unmotivated students will be forced into taking courses online.

Research suggests that when students who are not suited for online learning are forced into taking virtual courses, chances are high that they will either fail or drop out. Roblyer (1999, 2006; Roblyer et al., 2008; Roblyer & Marshall, 2002) has studied K–12 online learning dropouts and has found that the rates are comparable to or even worse than the dropout rates of online higher education students. Some of the lowest-performing virtual schools report dropout and failure rates as high as 60% to 70% of total school enrollment.

What K–12 Students Like and Dislike About Online Education

Another area of research on K–12 online learning focuses on better understanding students' feelings toward online instruction. Several studies have surveyed students after taking online courses and found similar results. Based on these studies (e.g., Barbour, 2008; Dewstow & Wright, 2005; Journell, 2010; Kapitzke & Pendergast, 2005; Tunison & Noonan, 2001), students generally seemed to enjoy the following about online learning:

- Autonomy of learning at their own pace, specifically, being able to work ahead
- Virtual teachers who were "nicer" and "less pushy" than classroom teachers
- Being able to e-mail their teachers with questions

When it came to their instructors, students across the board preferred teachers who were organized and well versed in their content areas as opposed to teachers who happened to be technologically savvy.

When asked to define negative aspects of their online courses, students were able to generate a more comprehensive list. The following were identified by students as negatively contributing to their online experience:

- Problems with technology
- Lack of time to complete assignments
- Difficulty understanding the goals/objectives of the course
- Difficulty finding information needed to complete assignments
- Lack of personal interaction with teacher and peers
- Not being able to get in contact with the teacher
- Slow Internet connections
- Poor time management
- Threaded discussion boards
- The amount of reading they had to do for assignments

Interestingly, the students in Tunison and Noonan's (2001) study also cited the autonomy to work at their own pace as the top disadvantage to online instruction. Perhaps not surprisingly, these students also frequently listed "poor time management" as a concern.

In my own research, I have found that another challenge associated with K–12 online learning is the perceptions of online instruction that students bring with them to their courses. In one study, students repeatedly admitted that they chose to take U.S. history online because they assumed it would be easier and would require less engagement with content than taking the course in a face-to-face environment. They also did not view their teacher or their peers as essential to their learning experience. In other words, they viewed their online course as completely self-directed learning in which they acquired and disseminated information in a way that simply satisfied a state requirement (Journell, 2010).

What K–12 Teachers Think About Online Learning

Fewer studies exist on K–12 teachers' attitudes toward online learning. As with their students, research suggests that teachers enjoy the flexibility of online instruction, especially in terms of being able to travel while remaining in touch with students. However, teachers also admit to experiencing a sharp learning curve the first time they attempt to move their curriculum online. For many online teachers, they find that they need to plan more thoroughly and be even more organized than in their face-to-face classes (Dewstow & Wright, 2005).

In that same study of the online U.S. history course, I found that the teacher shared many of his students' perceptions about online instruction. He believed that his students were taking the course only because they viewed the online format as the path of least resistance (he happened to be correct), and as a result, he did not expect much engagement from them. Like his students, he did not see the need for them to interact with each other online.

The teacher also did not seem to value teacher-student interaction. Although he regularly made himself available for students' questions via e-mail, he rarely tried to engage them in conversations about history. He also admitted that he watered down his curriculum when he taught online, at least compared with what he regularly did in his face-to-face classroom, because he did not know how to recreate the student-centered learning that he used in his classroom (Journell, 2008). His experience highlights the need for K–12 teachers to be trained in online pedagogy before they are asked to teach a virtual class.

WHAT CAN WE LEARN FROM RESEARCH ON K–12 ONLINE EDUCATION?

Overall, much of what has been written about instructional practices in K–12 online learning tends to mirror what one would find in any generic manual on teaching. For example, DiPietro, Ferdig, Black, & Preston (2008) surveyed and observed teachers from the Michigan Virtual School and created a comprehensive list of best practices for K–12 virtual schoolteachers. Other than the sections on building and sustaining community and technological proficiency, little of what was listed was unique to online education.

All teachers, regardless of the medium, need strong pedagogical content knowledge (Shulman, 1987), organization, classroom presence, awareness of learning differences, knowledge of assessments, and so on. In a sense, it is not complicated. Again, good teaching is good teaching, regardless of context.

Why, then, do we continue to read accounts of poor online experiences, even in courses taught by highly qualified and successful (at least in terms of their face-to-face instruction) teachers? The answer is simple. Most of the characteristics of good instruction look very different in the online classroom.

Take, for example, leading a discussion. All successful discussions, whether online or in a traditional classroom, involve teacher monitoring and feedback, an open forum for the give and take of ideas, and respect for diverse opinions. In a face-to-face classroom, however, teachers can see their students, which allows them to look for raised hands, expressions of confusion or boredom, or the quiet student who is itching to speak but needs to be coaxed into it. A threaded discussion board does not allow for any of these often subconscious tactics used by classroom teachers on a daily basis.

Yet it is certainly possible to expect teachers to engage their students in lively, student-centered instruction online as long as they are given the necessary tools and trained on how to use them. My aim is to identify those tools and then provide guidance on how to maximize their potential. The remainder of this book will offer practical suggestions on how to develop successful online learning environments designed specifically for K–12 learners.

SUMMARY

It is certainly possible that some readers might come away from this chapter feeling bleak about the prospects of teaching online. But the story of online K–12 education in the United States is still being written. Understanding the long history of distance education and the ongoing growing pains of online higher education can help place this current iteration of "anytime, anywhere" learning into context. The only difference, however, is that technology is improving at such a rapid pace that if districts and their teachers do not make an effort to stay ahead of the learning curve, they will fall behind.

If readers are to take anything from the history of online learning, it is this: online learning is here to stay. Is it perfect? No. But failing to reach perfection has yet to stop an educational mandate from being implemented, especially when it is thought to save money. So instead of fighting the change, skeptics need to realize that standing in front of a moving train is as unproductive as it is foolish. Rather, we need to embrace online education as a viable alternative to face-to-face instruction and begin preparing for the virtual classrooms of the 21st century.

NOTES

1. The problem with writing about technology is that it is constantly changing, and in order to stay abreast of new developments, one must read the most up-to-date research. Therefore, I would encourage interested readers to consider subscribing to journals that focus on online education. A few of the more popular ones are *Journal of Online Learning and Teaching*, which can be accessed for free at http://jolt.merlot.org/, *Journal of Interactive Online Learning*, which can be accessed for free at www.ncolr.org/jiol/, *American Journal of Distance Education*, *Distance Education*, *E-Learning and Digital Media*, *Journal of Computer-Mediated Communication*, and *Journal of Asynchronous Learning Networks*. The focus of many of these journals is on educational implications of online instruction in higher education or professional development programs as opposed to K–12 education. However, until the research base on K–12 online education improves, much of what we know about online learning will continue to be gleaned from these other contexts.

2. This section relies heavily on comprehensive reviews by Larreamendy-Joerns and Leinhardt (2006) and Moore (2003). Readers interested in specific details of these early distance education programs should access the references included in these reviews.

3. As an aside, I often use a video from a 1994 episode of *The Today Show* to hammer this point home with students; the video, which can be found at http://www.youtube.com/watch?v=hWX56YyyWKU, shows the hosts absolutely bewildered by the Internet.

4. This is not to say that there are no online K–12 education programs elsewhere in the world. Other countries have been found to offer online courses or programs in K–12 education; however, the vast majority of virtual schools and research on online learning in K–12 environments has taken place in the United States and Canada (Barbour & Reeves, 2009).

Chapter One

Creating a Proper Infrastructure for Online Learning

K–12 districts wishing to create online opportunities for their students have several options. The easiest way is to join an established collaborative, such as the Virtual High School, or encourage students to take classes through a state virtual high school. The problem with these options, however, is that districts and their teachers have little control over the curriculum or quality of instruction in these courses, and just as with face-to-face courses, the quality can vary from institution to institution. The only way, then, teachers can have a say in how online courses are created and implemented is to develop them on their own.

Online courses that are created and taught by district teachers and are monitored and assessed by district or school administrators are the fastest growing K–12 online programs in the United States (Watson et al., 2011). Yet for those attempting to create an online course from scratch, it can be a daunting proposition. The purpose of this chapter is to offer recommendations for those considering creating online courses in their districts or wishing to make improvements to existing courses.[1]

MAKING THE MOVE ONLINE

The first question that teachers need to ask themselves is whether they wish to move courses online. If the answer is "yes," then they are faced with a host of additional questions, such as

- Which courses will be offered online?

- Will the courses be totally online or a hybrid of face-to-face and online meetings?
- Will face-to-face alternatives be offered for online courses?
- Will the courses be offered during the regular school year or only in the summer?
- Will any student who wishes to take the courses be allowed to?
- How will students be prepared to take online courses?
- What should these courses look like?
- Will the courses be totally asynchronous, or will they involve synchronous class meetings?
- Will the courses be created from freely available technologies or from commercially licensed vendors?
- What will be the minimum and maximum enrollments in the courses?
- How will courses fit into existing district rules and regulations?
- How will teachers be expected to involve parents or guardians in their students' online experience?

As one can see, the decision to move online requires quite a bit of planning. Although any change in instruction involves a certain number of growing pains, if teachers can develop answers to these questions in the planning stages rather than react to problems after courses have been launched, the transition will be much smoother.

HOW TO CHOOSE WHICH COURSES ARE BEST SUITED FOR ONLINE LEARNING

When deciding which courses to move online, there are a number of factors to consider. At the top of the list should be whether the subject lends itself to online learning. Many "traditional" classes, such as health, language arts, or U.S. government, may be ideal for an online curriculum because those courses are often text and discussion based. Yet an anatomy class that requires students to dissect animals might be considerably more difficult to replicate online.

The bottom line is that the first question teachers should ask before moving a course online is whether the *learning objectives* of the course would be compromised in an online format. If not, then the course is a candidate to be moved online. If so, then teachers may decide that a hybrid approach (a combination of face-to-face and online meetings) may be more appropriate.

Another consideration in determining which courses should be moved online is student demand. Online courses are a great way for districts to offer courses with limited demand to a broader audience. Assume for a moment that an elective SAT preparation course has low enrollments at each of a district's three high schools. A district-wide online SAT preparation course would allow students from all three high schools to take the course, which would provide adequate enrollment without having to pay multiple teachers or forcing a single teacher to spend half of his or her day driving between campuses.

Conversely, teachers could use online courses to reduce the number of students in overcrowded classrooms in classes with high student demand. Offering sections of a class online siphons off students from face-to-face classes, leaving a more desirable student-to-teacher ratio. The students who choose to take the course online also receive the flexibility of completing their studies outside of normal school hours, freeing their schedules to take other classes or work more hours at their jobs.

In general, the literature supports hybrid courses over totally online formats because many students, especially adolescents, crave immediate feedback and instructor presence. Yet hybrid courses come at a cost. Whenever students are required to attend face-to-face sessions, courses lose a bit of the "anytime, anywhere" aspect that is part of the draw of online learning. Moreover, hybrid courses require additional resources (e.g., classroom space, personnel) that would not be needed were the courses totally online. Although there is no "right" answer to whether to move courses online, this decision needs to be made with care since teachers will be working with a population that may be unfamiliar with self-directed learning.

PROVIDING STUDENTS WITH CHOICES AND HELPING ENSURE THEIR SUCCESS

Students Should Be Given Face-to-Face and Online Options

Consider the following scenario: a student fails a regular-level English course due to a combination of poor reading ability and an inability to keep up with coursework (unorganized, regularly does not turn in homework, etc.). This student is a senior who needs this English course in order to graduate on time, and, unfortunately, the only option available to him during the second semester is a section of advanced placement English. Without a regular-level English option, the student's guidance counselor enrolls him in the advanced placement course and hopes for the best.

Although this scenario is hypothetical, hopefully most readers would consider forcing a student who struggled in a regular-level course into an advanced placement course not a good idea. Given that the reasons the student failed the regular-level course were that he could not read at grade level and did not appear motivated to study or complete homework, the chances of his succeeding in an advanced placement course are slim. In other words, it would be foolish to think that the outcome would be different simply because the student is told he has no other option and must do well in the advanced placement course in order to graduate.

Yet districts and schools often use this way of thinking when moving courses online. As students are given more online options, face-to-face options tend to fade away over time. Many students, as a result, are forced into a learning environment for which they are unsuited, and not surprisingly, many of them have poor experiences.

Research has shown that success in online courses requires specific academic strengths and dispositions. Namely, students should be above-average readers and writers, and they need to possess high levels of intrinsic motivation due to the self-directed aspect of online learning. Although these characteristics are important for online learners of any age, identifying potential motivational issues is crucial for K–12 programs.

Educational psychologists have identified motivation and self-regulation as traits that often grow stronger as students get older (Fox & Riconscente, 2008). These dispositions, therefore, may be a weakness for some adolescent learners that may cause them to respond to online learning considerably differently from their higher education counterparts. For students who do not possess the dispositions required to complete academic work on their own, online learning can have disastrous consequences.

Therefore, teachers should offer online and face-to-face options whenever possible and especially for required courses. In those cases where a lack of demand would not constitute giving students a choice between the two options, the courses designated for online delivery should be electives designed for advanced students. Students who sign up for advanced classes will most likely (but not always) have the dispositions and academic ability necessary for success in an online environment. In any case, teachers should make a conscious effort to put students in an environment in which they are most likely to be successful based on their academic strengths and weaknesses.

Students Need to Be Prepared for Online Learning

A problem arises when both online and face-to-face options are offered and students who do not possess the dispositions required for success online choose virtual courses simply because they do not want to come to school or they think online learning will be easier than face-to-face instruction. This is a common perception of adolescent learners, many of whom do not have prior experience with online learning. At this point, teachers must make the decision of whether to let these at-risk students enroll in online courses or force them to remain in the classroom.

As with traditional schooling, it is probably impossible for teachers or even administrators to keep students from taking a certain course if they (or their parents) really want to. Those in charge of online courses have a responsibility, however, to offer counseling to students who wish to take online courses. A frank discussion of students' chances for success online are especially important before their first online experience.

In her work, Roblyer (1999; Roblyer & Davis, 2008; Roblyer et al., 2008; Roblyer & Marshall, 2002) has attempted to develop a quantitative measure that will help predict adolescents' level of success in online courses. Below is the truncated version of the Educational Success Prediction Instrument that she developed and has used in various studies of K–12 online learning.

This survey touches on four categories of skills and dispositions that have been identified by research as necessary for success in online environments. Although the survey has been found to be a fairly reliable predictor of student success and failure in online courses, Roblyer has concluded that it probably best serves as a model for initiating conversations with students about what is required of online learning.[2]

This survey is not meant to be the perfect instrument to gauge student success online. Rather, it is an example of an early intervention procedure that could act as an objective starting point for students to think about what it will take to be successful in an online course. Teachers could easily develop their own surveys that would serve the same purpose.

Regardless of the instrument, the key is the discussion that occurs afterward. Teachers or other personnel should confer with students after taking this type of survey, and if students score poorly on one or more sections, they should be counseled accordingly. At the end of the day, it remains the students' decision whether to enroll in an online course. However, they should make that decision only after a frank assessment of their abilities and dispositions in comparison with those required for successful online learning.

SYNCHRONOUS VERSUS ASYNCHRONOUS COMMUNICATION

Once courses have been designated to be moved online, the next step is to determine the functionality of these courses. Obviously, the end goal is to replicate (or improve on) the learning outcomes that would have occurred in a face-to-face setting. Before launching into the types of platforms that are available to support K–12 online programs, it is necessary to first engage in a philosophical discussion of the ideal online learning environment.

Technically, one can engage in online learning by compiling a list of tasks online and then having students e-mail the completed tasks back to their teacher for assessment purposes. This approach, however, differs little from the postal correspondence courses of the late 19th century and does little to replicate the interactive, constructivist learning that is (hopefully) occurring in our 21st-century classrooms. If teachers want their online learning courses

Table 1.1. The Educational Success Prediction Instrument

Technology skills/
access/self-efficacy

1. I know how to locate a document or a program on my computer.
2. I know how to use a browser to locate Internet sites.
3. I feel comfortable using a computer.
4. I know how to use an Internet search engine to locate information.
5. I have easy access to a computer with Internet capability.
6. I have a computer in my home.
7. I know how to send an attachment in an e-mail.
8. I use e-mail or instant messaging at least once a week.
9. I have good word processing skills.
10. When I have to do something new on a computer, I usually try to figure it out myself.

Achievement beliefs

1. Many times, I lose interest in attaining the goals I set.
2. I rarely set goals for myself.
3. I believe I am a high achiever.
4. I find that I try harder if I set high goals for myself.
5. I study hard for all of my classes because I enjoy acquiring new knowledge.
6. I tend to persist at tasks until they are accomplished.

Instructional risk taking

1. I do not care what other people think of me if I make mistakes.
2. I am not afraid of making mistakes if I am learning to do new things.
3. I like taking chances and performing risky tasks in learning situations.
4. If I am given a task to perform that I know little about, I don't mind taking a chance.
5. When I am learning something new, it is okay if I make errors.
6. I am afraid of failure if I take risks.

Organization

1. I find it easier to study for an important test by breaking it into subparts rather than studying the whole subject matter at one time.
2. I keep my notes on each subject together and arranged in a logical order.
3. I will often set short-term goals to help me reach a long-term goal.

Source: Adapted from Roblyer et al., 2008.

to be socially constructivist in nature, then they must provide their students with ways in which to communicate with each other remotely.

The Benefits and Drawbacks of Asynchronous Communication

Perhaps the biggest decision that teachers must make, one that will ultimately shape how their online classes will operate, is whether their classes will be totally asynchronous or have synchronous components. Asynchronous communication is defined as "the exchange of messages in a medium that does not require the simultaneous presence of the sender and the receiver" (Bruce, 2004, p. 21). In other words, students and teachers can communicate with each other, but not in real time. Examples of asynchronous communication would be e-mail, threaded discussion boards, blogs, and wikis.

With asynchronous communication, there is always going to be a delay (even if both people are online at the same time) between when one participant makes a comment and when another participant replies to that comment. The beauty of asynchronous communication is that it allows participants to communicate with each other while still enjoying the "anytime, anywhere" aspect of online learning. In other words, participants do not need to be on their computers at the same time in order to engage in discussions of content, which research has found to be a major selling point for K–12 students (e.g., Journell, 2010; Tunison & Noonan, 2001).

Asynchronous communication has also been found to be effective for certain types of students (Hrastinski, 2008; Larson, 2003; Lyons, 2004):

- Shy students who do not typically participate in classroom conversations
- Students who may need more time to gather their thoughts in order to respond to their teachers and classmates
- Students who work well on their own

There is, however, a downside to asynchronous communication. Asynchronous conversations will always be choppy, and students who crave immediate feedback will be disappointed when they pose a question or comment on a discussion board and receive no response for hours or even days. Moreover, there is no guarantee that asynchronous posts will be read at all, especially when replies are not required or students feel as though there are too many posts to read (Journell, 2010).

The Benefits and Drawbacks of Synchronous Communication

Based on research on K–12 online learning in the United States and Canada, asynchronous communication is, by far, more prevalent than synchronous communication (Barbour, 2009; Murphy, Rodriguez-Manzanares, & Barbour, 2011). Synchronous communication is defined as "the exchange of messages in a medium that requires the simultaneous presence of the sender and receiver" (Bruce, 2004, p. 21). Activities such as talking with others in chat rooms, on instant messenger programs, via telecommunication (e.g., Skype), or even via phone conferencing would be examples of synchronous communication.

The obvious downside to synchronous communication is that it takes away from the flexibility afforded by online learning. Students who take online courses primarily because they wish to fit their academic responsibilities around their work and personal needs may find synchronous requirements cumbersome. Certainly, students' flexibility needs to be considered when districts decide on the format of their online curricula, but it should not be the only consideration.

Research has found that synchronous communication offers teachers and students the following benefits (e.g., Boling, Hough, Krinsky, Saleem, & Stevens, 2012; Haythornthwaite & Bregman, 2004; Hrastinski, 2008; Journell et al., 2013; Levin et al., 2006; Mabrito, 2006):

- The environment is more authentic and closer to that they would find in a traditional classroom situation.
- Discussions are more productive, and the conversation moves at a much faster pace.
- Similarities to face-to-face conversations promote a sense of community among students.
- Students receive immediate feedback to ideas.

There are also limitations to synchronous communication. In particular, students can find the speed of synchronous conversations, especially when using text-based chat programs, to be overwhelming. For slow typists and students who wish to thoughtfully compose responses, synchronous chats often move at a pace that causes them to fall behind (e.g., Hou & Wu, 2011). One way to circumvent that problem is to use synchronous video software. This type of software allows users to simulate a face-to-face classroom experience through the use of microphones and webcams so that users can see and hear each other in real time.

Merging Synchronous and Asynchronous Communication as a Best Practice

In summary, synchronous and asynchronous modes of communication each have pedagogical strengths and weaknesses. Therefore, teachers should incorporate a balance between the two modes of communication when they plan the structure of their online courses. Teachers can use asynchronous modes of communication to allow students to reflect on complex issues while still maintaining the "anytime, anywhere" component of online learning. They can also provide regular opportunities for synchronous communication to increase the sense of community among students and allow for immediate feedback on assignments or discussions related to content.

An ideal balance would be something like having one synchronous chat session per week, held at a consistent time. Teachers would be able to have their entire class "present" to tie up loose ends, explain upcoming assignments, or discuss issues pertaining to content. Too many synchronous class meetings, however, would probably restrict students' flexibility and disrupt the reason that many of them chose to take an online class in the first place.

If, however, synchronous sessions are limited to one or two per week and held at consistent times, students should be able to work around them. The bottom line is that teachers must manage the persistent conflict between maintaining flexibility and ensuring that learning objectives are being met. The way teachers structure this balance will be instrumental in determining the type of learning management system they need in order to implement their pedagogical vision.

CHOOSING A LEARNING MANAGEMENT SYSTEM

Free Software

In this day and age, creating websites is easier than ever before. Until recently, most website development required considerable knowledge of instructional design and familiarity with pricey site-creation software, such as FrontPage or Dreamweaver. Now, anyone with a Google account and basic computer skills can create websites almost instantaneously. Other websites, such as Wix.com or Weebly.com, also offer free, step-by-step site-creation programs that involve minimal technological know-how.

Before any readers get too excited about the cost-saving potential of these free site-creation options, it is important to note that they have significant limitations when considering them as platforms for online learning. They are great for creating personal websites or portfolios that only convey information and provide hyperlinks for readers to access outside material. However, they provide no outlet for turning in assignments (other than via e-mail), and they offer no option, synchronous or asynchronous, for students to communicate with each other.

The better option, then, is to use a learning management system (LMS) specifically designed for education. Again, low-cost options are available. Edmodo (www.edmodo.com) and Moodle (www.moodle.org) are examples of free LMSs that can be accessed online or downloaded for use in classrooms.

Although these programs are an upgrade over self-made websites, both in terms of appearance and functionality, they still have limitations. Both Edmodo and Moodle offer teachers options for asynchronous communication but are limited in terms of their synchronous applications (Edmodo uses a structure similar to that of Facebook while Moodle uses a classic threaded discussion-board format). The reason for the omission of synchronous technologies in these LMSs is simple: they are more expensive to create, often require more bandwidth, and are not essential to the purpose for which these systems were created.

Both Edmodo and Moodle were designed to enhance blended or face-to-face instruction. According to the Moodle website, "a hybrid, blended model of courses where Moodle simply supports and/or extends the face-to-face and other activities is by far the most widely used way of using Moodle by teachers and students worldwide" (Moodle, 2012). This is not to say, however, that districts could not use a platform like Edmodo or Moodle for totally online courses (the Open University in Britain, for example, uses Moodle as its primary course-delivery option), but it does mean that districts would potentially have to sacrifice some of the benefits of synchronous communication.

It is possible, of course, to find synchronous chat rooms for free on the Internet or through free LMS. These chat rooms or instant messenger programs would allow students to "meet" in the same place with their teacher and, theoretically, engage in "classroom" discussions. However, anyone who has ever participated in a chat room knows that trying to carry on a conversation with a handful of people is difficult, much less in a class of more than 20 students.

New technologies are emerging that offer hope for teachers wishing to utilize more engaging synchronous tools in their courses free of charge. Google+ now offers a "hangout" feature that allows users to meet virtually using webcams and microphones. In theory, this program would eliminate the need to purchase a commercial LMS because it simulates the type of synchronous experience found in those types of for-profit programs. Teachers and students can see each other via webcam and talk to each other in real time with their microphones.

Unfortunately, this technology has limitations. The program has limited bandwidth, and only a handful of people can use their webcams and microphones at the same time. Yet Google+ is likely the first in a wave of free synchronous applications, and the technology will only improve over time.

Commercial Learning Management Systems

Research shows that most K–12 districts that have online programs use commercial vendors, such as Blackboard or Canvas (Conceição & Drummond,

2005). Although teachers rarely have influence over monetary decisions made by their school or district, access to commercial LMSs can greatly enhance the quality of students' online experiences. A detailed discussion of the cost of these types of programs is beyond the scope of this book, but Figure 1.1 gives some rough figures for a couple of popular LMSs. Teachers interested in moving courses online should advocate for the purchase of a polished LMS whenever possible.

For the purposes of this discussion, let's assume that teachers have access to a commercial LMS. This type of program offers teachers a wide range of tools for online instruction, including applications for non-text-based synchronous meetings. Figure 1.2 shows a screenshot of Blackboard Collaborate, which is Blackboard's current option for synchronous course meetings.

The system allows for microphones and webcams. Either students would need to have these items provided for them, or they would need to acquire them on their own. Many laptops come equipped with built-in webcams and microphones, but if that is not an option, a decent webcam with a built-in microphone can be purchased for around $35.

The window at the top left provides a small screen for webcam views, which teachers can turn on or off at their leisure. Being able to show webcam

---

The Cost of Commercial Vendors

Purchasing a commercial LMS requires a sizeable portion of a district's budget. License fees for commercial vendors are often predicated on the total number of students enrolled in a district and the type of package needed to meet their instructional goals. In writing this book, I attempted to contact Blackboard for a pricing guideline, but they refused to discuss monetary figures.

For a frame of reference, I contacted a school district in Virginia that used Blackboard for both online and face-to-face courses. The district has an enrollment of approximately 14,000 students, and the total cost of their site license (which included a mid-range package) came to approximately $225,000 for the 2012-2013 school year.

Blackboard is considered the goal standard when discussing LMS. However, newer companies are attempting to break into the market. One such company is Canvas (www.instructure.com), and their pricing system is more straightforward. Their fees range between $9 and $17 per student and is based on the total enrollment in the district. Based on a conversation with a Canvas representative, a district of 13,000 students would pay approximately $151,000 per year, while a district of 73,000 students would pay approximately $657,000 per year.

This may seem like a steep price for some school districts. However, qualifying districts can apply to the federal government for assistance. The E-rate program sponsored by the Schools and Library section of the Universal Service Administrative Company, which is overseen by the Federal Communication Commission, allows districts to apply for reductions of site license fees for educational software programs, including LMS. Interested readers can refer to http://www.usac.org for more information

---

Figure 1.1. The Cost of Commercial Vendors

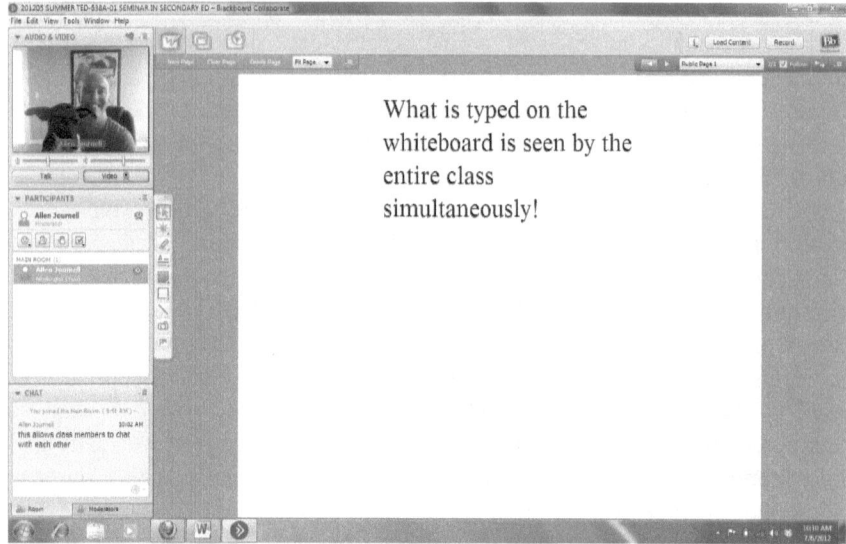

Figure 1.2. The Blackboard Collaborate Screen for Synchronous Communication

views allows students to see each other or, at the very least, their teacher. These visuals provide students with a greater sense of classroom presence by offering a glimpse into the personalities of their classmates and teachers (for example, one might be able to conclude that I am an animal lover because I included my dog, Parker, in my camera shot).

Depending on bandwidth, one or multiple participants can speak at a time through their microphones so that the whole class can hear them. It would be unproductive, however, if everyone were speaking at the same time, so the program offers teachers the option of having students "raise their hands" as they would in a face-to-face classroom. Students would press the button with a hand symbol (located in the middle box on the left side of the screen) when they wished to speak and then would wait to be recognized by the teacher. Other students can voice their pleasure or displeasure about what is being said by clicking on the appropriate emoticon, which would then appear beside their name.

The program also supports a chat feature, which is located at the bottom left of the screen. Although chats by themselves are problematic, when used alongside audio conversations, they can actually enhance classroom communication. Research has shown that students instinctively begin using the chat function without being told, and while the academic discussion is occurring through the speakers, the informal conversations that serve to build community and social presence are being held in the chat window (Journell et al., 2013). The use of both the chat and audio creates a richer experience than even what one would find in a face-to-face classroom (Debuse, Hede, & Lawley, 2009; Moreno & Mayer, 2002).

The most prominent feature of Blackboard Collaborate is the large whiteboard in the middle of the screen. What makes the whiteboard such an effective pedagogical tool is that whatever is written can be seen simultaneously by the other members of the class. In this sense, the whiteboard acts similar to a Google Docs application. Similarly, teachers can upload PowerPoint presentations and other visuals, including videos, which could then be viewed by the entire class simultaneously.

If teachers wish to put their students into small groups, similar to the way they would in a face-to-face classroom, they can use the "breakout rooms." In their breakout rooms, students have their own whiteboard and can speak to each other through their microphones. In other words, the rest of the class cannot see or hear what they are doing (although the teacher can enter any of the breakout rooms at any time). When the activity has ended, the teacher can eliminate the breakout rooms, and all of the students come back to the main classroom page to share what they did in their smaller groups.

These are just a sampling of the features offered by programs such as Blackboard Collaborate. Other instructional tools include:

- The ability for teachers to send their students on a guided Internet tour in which the teacher shares what is on his or her screen with students
- The ability to record the entire session (chat, video, and audio) so that it can be viewed at a later date or given to students who had to miss the session
- A polling feature that allows students to answer questions simultaneously and anonymously
- A timer to monitor time spent on activities or in group work
- The ability to enroll individuals from outside of the class to serve as guest speakers

As one can see, this type of synchronous tool mimics much of what students would find in a typical face-to-face classroom. This type of program is essential for taking the distance out of online learning and fostering a social constructivist approach in a virtual classroom. Whenever possible, teachers should advocate for the purchase of a quality synchronous LMS in order to meet the learning needs of their students.

ADDITIONAL INFRASTRUCTURE ISSUES RELATED TO ONLINE COURSES

The format of online learning creates several logistical headaches as teachers and students attempt to reconcile virtual instruction with existing district policies. Most district policies are written for students in traditional schools who are learning from teachers in face-to-face classrooms. Online learning will force teachers to revamp many of their existing practices.

Teachers Need to Develop Professional Communication With Students

Online courses by nature require communication between teachers and students via e-mail and other electronic means. Unfortunately, the highly publicized actions of a few unprofessional teachers in recent years have prompted many districts and even a few states to adopt strict policies regarding private electronic communication between teachers and students. In 2011, for example, Missouri passed a law banning such communication, and New York City passed similar legislation a year later (Chen & McGeehan, 2012; Peterson, 2011).

Many of these laws and policies were meant to target teachers who befriend their students on social media programs such as Facebook or Twitter. When going by the letter of the law, however, they prohibit e-mail communication as well. Given the importance of e-mail communication in online learning, teachers must develop policies to protect themselves from potential sexual harassment, inappropriate relationships, or frivolous lawsuits.

One option would be for teachers to send all e-mails to students using their district e-mail accounts. Teachers should never use personal e-mail accounts to communicate with students. Moreover, it is good practice to have all e-mails sent to students copied to a generic district account. This way, administrators can be privy to all course-related e-mails being sent to students, which would provide protection and documentation for teachers.

This type of policy, however, would not necessarily allow districts to monitor students' e-mails to teachers. If students do not have e-mail accounts provided to them by the district, teachers should have students create generic e-mail accounts to use only for academic purposes. These e-mail addresses should be professional (an easy option would be to have students create a free e-mail account with their full name, such as wayne_journell@gmail.com). HotStuff69@yahoo.com might be fine for a student to use with his or her friends, but it is asking for trouble when used to e-mail a teacher.

Of course, no amount of caution can keep bad things from happening online. After all, nothing is stopping teachers and students from e-mailing each other using personal accounts. Being diligent in monitoring e-mail communication, however, can help teachers cover their backsides when something inappropriate does occur.

At the very least, online teachers need to be aware of the potential dangers of communicating with adolescents via e-mail and take steps to protect themselves from unsubstantiated allegations from students. As in traditional schooling, the key to protecting oneself is to document, document, and then document some more. If teachers cannot produce evidence, it comes down to their word versus the student's word, and even if the teacher is innocent, he or she will often lose in the court of public opinion.

How to Assess Students' Attendance Online

A problem specific to K–12 online education is how to handle truancy and tardiness online. Truancy laws differ from state to state, but most require compulsory attendance unless excused by a parent or guardian. In a traditional setting, determining absences is fairly easy; students are either present or they are not. If students are absent a certain number of days, a series of procedures (letters home, meetings with parents, etc.) occurs until the students reach a threshold where they fail or are automatically held back a year. Most districts have similar policies related to tardiness, with punishments ranging from detention to suspension or failure.

Assessing attendance and tardiness is considerably more challenging online. Obviously, synchronous sessions are fairly easy—students either log in or they do not. But how can teachers determine attendance in an asynchronous, "anytime, anywhere" environment? Bender (2010), an administrator for an online high school in Minnesota, describes a method in which the percentage of student work completed is converted to an attendance policy.

For example, if students complete 35% or more of their work for that week, they were considered "present" for that week (this is not to say that they did all of their work or did it well, rather that they did enough work to be considered in good attendance). If students complete 10% of their work, however, they are given three absences for the week, and if they complete only 5% of their work, they are given four absences. Then, teachers follow established district policies based on the total number of absences (e.g., letters sent home, truancy petitions to the district, etc.).

Bender's (2010) approach is only one example of a truancy policy, and it may not work for every teacher. The larger point is that teachers need to consider these policies *before* implementing online programs. If not, students will quickly learn to cut whatever corners they can and force the issue, regardless.

The Need for Parent Involvement

Another issue unique to K–12 online learning is how to encourage parental involvement in online courses. Some parents may not have e-mail addresses or be proficient with technology. Teachers need to decide how they can most effectively contact these parents, and vice versa, if there are concerns about a student's performance in an online course.

Also, teachers need policies for aspects of traditional schooling that allow parents to meet face-to-face with their children's teachers. For example, if an online course is not affiliated with a school, then how can a parent attend a "back-to-school night?" Similarly, if a course is open to students throughout a district, it could make scheduling meetings with parents challenging.

These types of policies become even more significant when one accounts for research on the importance of parental involvement to students' success in online courses. Recent research suggests that parental involvement may be even more important for online students than those in face-to-face classrooms because of the large amount of time students spend learning at home (Liu, Black, Algina, Cavanaugh, & Dawson, 2010). It is imperative, therefore, that teachers create policies that allow online parents to play an integral part in their children's education.

How to Determine Ideal Enrollment for Online Courses

Teachers also need to establish parameters for online enrollments. K–12 classrooms typically average anywhere from 20 to 30 students, and many teachers and administrators assume that online courses can handle the same number of students (or more). Research suggests, however, that online instruction actually creates *more* work for teachers than face-to-face instruction and requires them to spend more time grading and communicating with students. Therefore, most scholars recommend that online enrollments not exceed 15 students (e.g., Conceição, 2006; DiBiase, 2000, 2004; Kapitzke & Pendergast, 2005; Tomei, 2006).

Ideal class sizes, of course, are rarely attained in public education. It is important to note, though, that teachers may exceed the amount of time spent on instructional tasks online than they do in their face-to-face classes. Teachers must remember that although they may be completing this work at home, there is still a finite amount of time that they can spend on their online courses. The more students enrolled, the less individual attention teachers can give students and the less time they can spend building classroom community and monitoring asynchronous communication.

The Importance of Establishing Systematic Evaluation Procedures

Finally, teachers must establish some form of quality control for their online instruction. In traditional schools, principals have developed methods for assessing teacher quality (observations, pop-in visits, student evaluations, etc.), but online courses may be an afterthought. Teachers need to be held accountable for student learning online just as they would be in a face-to-face course. Most LMSs such as Blackboard or Canvas allow teachers to enroll administrators as teaching assistants or guests. That way, administrators can sit in on synchronous sessions or monitor teachers' handling of threaded discussion boards.

Teachers would be wise to develop a method of distributing course evaluations for students, especially in the first years of an online course. Again, most LMS programs offer teachers the capability to give students anonymous surveys that allow students to be honest in their assessment of the course and their teachers' instruction. The key, of course, is to take these evaluations seriously. Students are often the best judge of a course's effectiveness, and even at the K–12 level, they are capable of providing useful feedback that teachers can use to improve the quality of their courses.

These examples are but a few of the considerations facing teachers as they make the move to online curricula. This list is far from comprehensive, but hopefully it spurs additional thought about necessary changes that have to be made prior to the creation of a course. Problems with infrastructure are never hidden for long, and issues will surely arise even among the best laid plans. The more teachers can anticipate, however, the less they will have to react to after the fact, which is always a formula for success.

SUMMARY

The act of moving courses online is complex. Numerous decisions have to be made before any students are enrolled, and all of them will affect the quality of instruction that occurs in these courses. To recap, here is a quick list of questions that need to be answered once teachers decide to move a course online:

- Will an online version of the course meet desired instructional goals?
- Will students be given a choice to take online or face-to-face versions of the course?
- How will students be counseled on what is needed for success in online courses?
- Will the course contain both synchronous and asynchronous forms of communication?
- What type of LMS will be needed to meet desired instructional goals?

- How will teachers effectively and appropriately communicate with their online students?
- How will teachers accurately monitor student attendance online?
- How will teachers involve parents of their online students?
- What will be the minimum and maximum enrollments for the course?
- How will teachers ensure systematic evaluations of their courses?

NOTES

1. I recognize that many of the recommendations I make in this chapter may be beyond a teacher's control. Depending on their district administrative structure, teachers may not have a say in their online enrollments or what type of technology they use for their online courses. I pose these recommendations as a way of providing teachers with knowledge that they can share with district and school administrators.

2. In a personal correspondence with Margaret Roblyer as I was writing this chapter, she indicated that although the Educational Success Prediction Instrument has been a fairly reliable indicator of student success or failure, there are so many other variables that also influence those outcomes, at least at the secondary level. Therefore, she hesitates to use the survey as a prediction instrument but rather advocates using the content contained in the survey as a way of supporting students' online performance.

Chapter Two

Course Development

On the surface, creating online courses may not seem too difficult. After all, most prospective online teachers will have a wealth of resources that they already use in their face-to-face classes. Given the amount of digital technology used by today's classroom teachers and the relative low cost of scanners and digital cameras, it is certainly possible to upload just about everything that one uses in a face-to-face environment to an LMS. Yet just because teachers can make all of their materials available to students online does not mean that students can necessarily learn from them.

Especially for the novice online teacher, most of the lessons and materials that they use will have been created for face-to-face classrooms, where teachers are present to fill in any gaps that may exist. Creating a PowerPoint presentation for a classroom lecture, for example, is much different from creating one designed for students to read independently. In person, teachers can supplement their PowerPoint slides with anecdotes or by highlighting words of significance, but that is lost when students simply download a file and read it on their own.

Although most of the sound pedagogical strategies that teachers use in their face-to-face classes are the same online, teachers have to be cognizant of the differences between learning online and learning in classrooms. As a general rule, it is beneficial for teachers to run through their courses as students (or, better yet, have someone else do it) before launching the actual, real course in order to find any potential problems that may exist. Besides finding obvious glitches, such as broken links, exploring a course as a student will quickly highlight areas of conceptual confusion.

The reason that creating an online course is challenging is simple. It is difficult to train one's mind to think in terms of creating lessons for self-directed learning, especially when one is used to the immediacy of face-to-face instruction. The good news is that the vast amount of instructional technology that teachers have at their disposal narrows the gap between self-directed and classroom learning considerably.

This chapter will focus on creating a solid structure for learning online, one that allows students to learn on their own without ever feeling as though they are learning in isolation. Without a solid structure, however, students will grow frustrated and give up before true learning can take place. The key to successful online learning is minimizing the number of procedural and technical questions that can occur so that the focus can be on content.

HOW TO CREATE A SOLID COURSE STRUCTURE

A solid course structure is important for a successful online course. A consistent source of frustration for online students is being unable to find items needed to complete their assignments. If poor organization frustrates college students and adult learners, one can only imagine the reactions of adolescents who rarely spend more than thirty seconds looking for something before giving up or asking for help.

Course Layout

The layout of an online course should be clear and easy to navigate. When creating the shell of a course, a teacher's goal should be to never receive an e-mail from a student asking, "Where do I find [insert specific assignment/ reading/link here]?" The first step to creating an organized course lies in a clearly labeled, prominently visible navigational tool that allows students to jump from one section of the course to another.

Most LMSs allow teachers to customize the navigational tools in their courses. Although what is included in a navigation bar will often be course specific, several items should be common to all online courses:

- An announcements page where teachers can post time-sensitive announcements and reminders
- A link to a listing of the teacher's name, contact information, and times for virtual office hours
- A course information page that contains the syllabus, course calendar, and any course-specific procedures
- A page that lists all of the assignment descriptions and due dates
- A page containing all of the required course readings (these can also be listed in each respective unit)
- A link to the course discussion board or other form of asynchronous discussion being used in the course

- A link to the mode of synchronous communication being used in the course
- A "coffee house" where students can talk informally and ask questions about assignments
- A link to the online gradebook so that students can stay abreast of their progress in the course

Figure 2.1 provides an example from a course created by one of my graduate students using Blackboard technology:

Of course, no matter how clearly a course may be labeled, there will always be students who have difficulty navigating through it. English language learners and students who struggle with reading may become especially frustrated when trying to follow step-by-step text instructions. A strategy supported by the literature is meeting with online students face to face before the course starts to model how to access various aspects of the course.

An initial face-to-face meeting may not always be possible, however, and even if students are shown a procedure once, there is no guarantee that they will remember how to do it once they get home. Teachers, therefore, should develop directions for navigating their courses that students can access on their own. In order to cater to multiple learning styles, directions are most effective when provided in both text and multimedia formats. Text directions

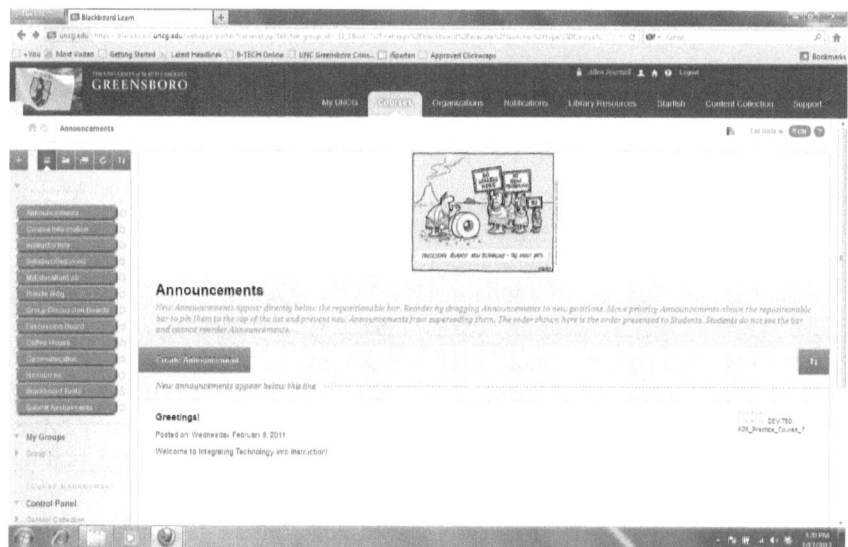

Figure 2.1. Announcements Page for Teacher Use

are self-explanatory, but for directions that incorporate video and audio components, screencasts are a useful tool.

Screencasts

A screencast is a recording of what a user does on his or her computer screen. Teachers can use screencast software to create a video narrated by audio that provides a step-by-step guide for how to do a particular task in the course. To see an example of a screencast that I created for how to post on a Blackboard discussion board, go to http://youtu.be/a3gAqkoidYU.

Almost any task that teachers require their students to do online can be made into a screencast. Take, for example, assignment submission. Let's say that a teacher is requiring all of his or her students to turn in assignments using the digital dropbox feature of Blackboard.

The teacher would turn on the screencast software and model the steps to turn in assignments on his or her computer while simultaneously describing the steps orally—starting with how to save a Word document to the desktop, then opening Blackboard, followed by navigating to the digital dropbox page, uploading the Word document as an attachment, and then clicking Submit. The result is a video that the teacher could then post directly on Blackboard or upload to YouTube for students to access.

Creating a screencast is simple. All one needs is a microphone and free screencast software, easily accessed online. Googling "how to make a screencast" will provide several options from which to choose, but Jing (http://www.techsmith.com/jing.html) is a good option because it works for both Macs and PCs. Once the free software is downloaded, all users need to do is click Record. At that point, the software should begin recording all actions that are being performed on the computer as well as any corresponding audio.

Once the screencast is finished, users should click the Stop button, and the software will offer the option to save the video to the computer. At that point, users can upload the video as they see fit. If the software forces users to save the video in a format that does not work on their or their students' computers, they can use additional free software to change the format of the video. To view a screencast on how to make screencasts using Jing, refer to http://www.youtube.com/watch?v=3EZktLorV3E.

One hint, though, about creating the audio for a screencast: It is helpful if users write out a script for the video beforehand. No matter how many times one may have done a certain task, it is easy to get "stage fright" and fumble one's words once the microphone turns on. At the very least, videos made without scripts tend to contain a lot of "ums" and other verbal ticks that can be distracting for those trying to follow along.

ESTABLISHING EFFECTIVE INSTRUCTIONAL DESIGN IN ONLINE COURSES

Organization is a hallmark of smoothly run online courses. Even more so than in a face-to-face environment, the planning and implementation of online instruction occurs before a single student enrolls. Given the nature of "anytime, anywhere" learning, it is not unusual for teachers to have an entire course completely planned, created, and ready to go prior to the first day of class. As opposed to a face-to-face class where a teacher may stay only a week (or less) ahead of his or her students, online teachers must be more prepared given that students are not always going to be working on the same assignment at the exact same time.

Instructional Planning

Instructional planning can be done in a variety of ways, but the same backward-design approach often used for traditional instruction works well within online environments (Wiggins & McTighe, 2005). This approach helps with both long- and short-term planning by encouraging teachers to focus on student learning outcomes and then determine how to effectively achieve these goals. Backward design is ideal for online learning because it requires structure.

Within a backward-design approach, teachers first look at their content broadly and then decide how to narrow it down into smaller, more manageable segments. Courses are broken into units, units into topics, topics into lessons, and lessons into activities based on learning objectives. Figure 2.2 shows an example of backward design for part of an American history course.[1]

The physical organization of an online course should reflect its instructional design. Teachers can use folders to make their instructional design easy to navigate. Figure 2.3 provides an example of this type of organization. In this course created by Miguel, one of my graduate students, the folders correspond with the units that make up the entirety of his course "The Citizen and American Politics." Each unit, or session, is designed to cover a week's worth of material, and students are expected to complete the sessions in sequential order based on the due dates provided in the course calendar.

In this example, Miguel has chosen to make all of his sessions available to students at the beginning of the course. That is a perfectly fine approach for classes in which students are encouraged to work at their own pace or if teachers do not care whether students look at the work they will be doing in upcoming units. In many cases, however, having students work ahead or preview upcoming material is not desirable. In these cases, the timing fea-

> **Course:** American History
>
> **Example of a Possible Unit:** The American Revolution
>
> **Example of a Possible Topic for Unit:** Colonists' response to British taxation efforts
>
> **Example of a Possible Lesson for Topic:** A lesson describing the Boston Tea Party
>
> **Example of a Possible Activities for Lesson:** An analysis of the painting "The Destruction of Tea at Boston Harbor", A webquest on the leaders of the protest, an asynchronous discussion board assignment requiring students to compare the Tea Party of 1773 and the political tea Party of 2013.

Figure 2.2. Backward Design in an American History Course

tures available in most LMSs would allow teachers to hide certain material until they want their students to access it.

Unit Design

Where students primarily engage with content is in the activities that each individual unit comprises. Before considering implications for developing content online, let's first consider the goals of instructional planning for a more familiar context—a face-to-face classroom. The primary goal of any lesson is to meet learning objectives, whether they are content or skill related. A secondary objective is to maintain order in the classroom, often by sticking to a familiar lesson structure for students.

Most classroom teachers find success in maintaining a regular routine. It is a good teaching practice, for example, to have students complete an opening activity, often called a "bellringer." For consistency, these bellringers should be posted in the same place each day so that students know where to look when they enter the classroom. The idea is that, with repeated practice, students will come to see the bellringers as routine and will eventually start their bellringers at the beginning of class without additional prodding from the teacher.

Although one of the perks to teaching online is that classroom management issues are minimized, the idea of keeping students in a routine is still valuable. The more consistent teachers can be in their learning activities, the better. Figure 2.4 provides an example from a course created by Melissa, another one of my graduate students.

Melissa chose to structure her course using a case-based approach, where students' interests are piqued by reading a fictional case about the topic to be discussed in the unit. In each unit, Melissa has made it clear to her students that the first thing they are to do is read the case for the week. Then, students

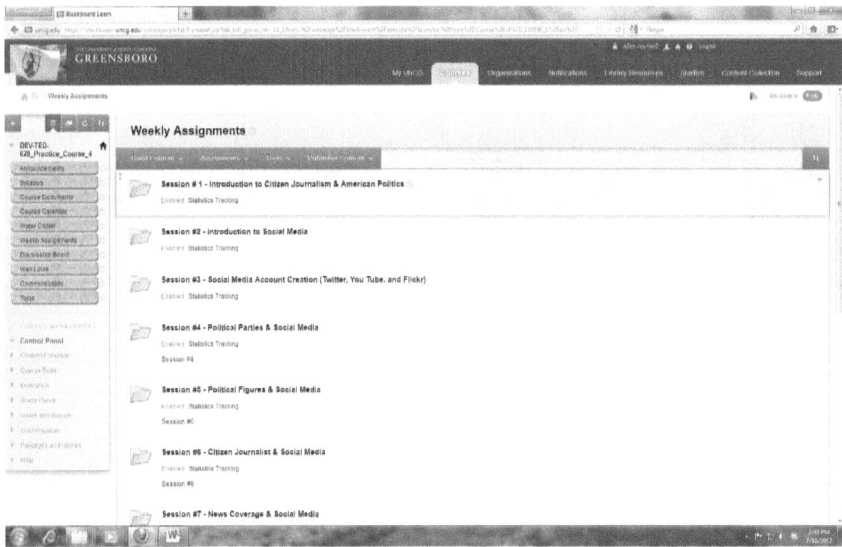

Figure 2.3. Weekly Assignments Organized by Session

are to read the required texts for the week, respond to a prompt on the discussion board, and then view examples of projects others have created before attempting to create their own and turn it in for a grade.

Each unit in Melissa's course follows the same pattern, the only exception being that she periodically mixes in a few synchronous class meetings. Once she models for her students how to complete the first unit, subsequent units will run smoothly because students will be familiar with the process. This level of consistency is important for online instruction because teachers are not physically present to answer questions students may have. Being consistent will provide structure and comfort to students, especially for those who may have learning disabilities or who may struggle with technology, and should minimize the number of e-mails teachers receive regarding procedural issues.

Instructional Activities

Determining the types of instructional activities to use in each unit will depend on the learning objectives in the course. A popular approach advocated in the online literature follows this basic pattern:

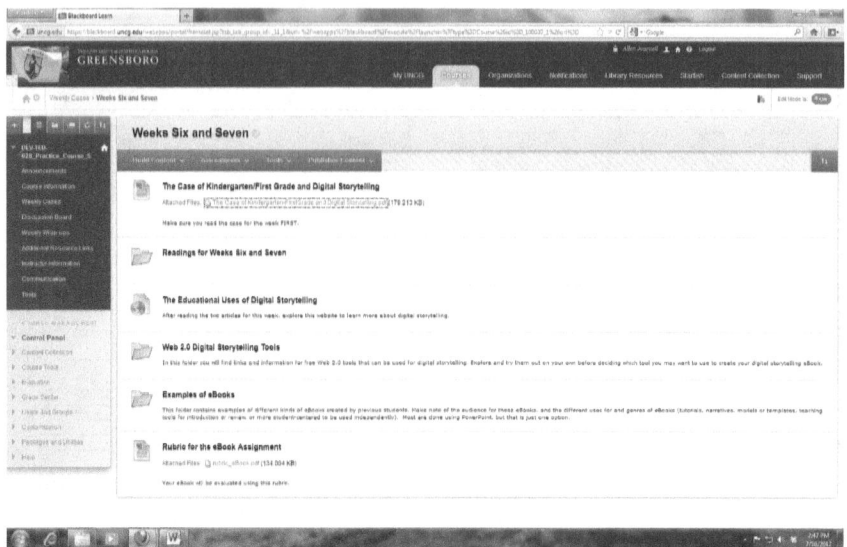

Figure 2.4. Organizing Activities Online

- *Activate prior knowledge*—an initial task that requires students to think about what they already know about a topic (e.g., KWL charts, journal entries, Venn diagrams, etc.)
- *Consult the experts*—sources where students acquire knowledge about the topic from respected authorities (e.g., textbook, teacher-made notes, websites, etc.)
- *Apply your knowledge*—activities in which students apply their newfound knowledge (e.g., webquests, experiments, graphic organizers, etc.)
- *Reflect on what you learned*—tasks that ask students to summarize what they have learned and apply that knowledge to past experiences, prior knowledge, or other topics (e.g., journal entries, completed KWL charts, etc.)

Although this approach follows a logical progression, it lacks a clear social component. This is not to say that one or more of the activities cannot incorporate opportunities for collaboration among peers, but it is not explicitly stated.

Horton (2006) offers another approach to unit design that focuses heavily on collaboration. In his design, each session starts with a synchronous class meeting where the instructor presents information and students can ask questions. Then, instructors post an assignment online and allow members of the class to discuss the assignment either synchronously or asynchronously. At that point, students complete the assignment and submit it to the instructor for grading.

There is no absolutely correct way to structure an online course, and much of the design will depend on the subject being taught. Horton's (2006) approach, for example, seems more appropriate for advanced courses, where students already have a basic grasp of content, whereas the first approach may be more appropriate for the survey nature of most K–12 courses. It is essential, however, for students to have regular opportunities to discuss content with their peers. K–12 courses, therefore, would be ideal for a hybrid of the two aforementioned approaches containing the following components:

- *Activate prior knowledge*—an initial task that requires students to think about what they already know about a topic (e.g., KWL chart, journal entries, Venn Diagrams, etc.)
- *Consult the experts*—sources where students acquire knowledge about the topic from respected authorities (e.g., textbook, teacher-made notes, websites, etc.)
- *Learn from others*—a formal discussion with peers about what has been learned from the experts (e.g., a teacher-prompted question on a threaded discussion board)
- *Apply your knowledge*—individual or group activities in which students apply what they have learned from the experts and each other (e.g., webquests, experiments, graphic organizers, etc.)
- *Reflect on what you learned*—tasks that ask students to summarize what they have learned and apply that knowledge to past experiences, prior knowledge, or other topics (e.g., journal entries, KWL charts, etc.)
- *Check for understanding*—a teacher-led meeting where teachers can assess whether learning objectives were met and students can share what they have learned from assignments and discussions (e.g., a synchronous class session)

With this structure, there is a nice balance of self-directed learning, teacher-directed learning, and peer-assisted learning. While online instruction is always going to contain an element of self-directed learning, it is important, especially with adolescents, to be sure that steps are taken to lessen feelings of isolation. Creating opportunities for interactions with peers and teachers will also go a long way toward building a classroom community.

SUMMARY

A solid structure is essential to a successful online learning experience. Using a backward-design approach helps teachers logically arrange units so that they are aligned with learning objectives. Within each unit of a course, students should have opportunities to both work independently and collaborate with others. The following approach is ideal for the learning needs of adolescent learners:

- Activating prior knowledge
- Consulting the experts
- Learning from others
- Applying your knowledge
- Reflecting on what you learned
- Checking for understanding

NOTE

1. For an extensive discussion of using backward design in online courses, see Horton, 2006.

Chapter Three

Assessing Student Learning Online

As in the classroom, the focus in an online course should be on engagement, not just memorization of content. Remember, good teaching is good teaching, regardless of the medium! Many readers may be thinking about their own classroom instruction and immediately jump to that favorite lesson that they cannot fathom working in an online format. That is a natural reaction to have, especially the first time one is faced with moving curricula online.

With some creativity, most face-to-face activities can be adapted for use in online courses. Even if they cannot, however, the opportunity afforded by being able to plan instruction knowing that all students will have unfettered access to the Internet may provide alternatives that, in many cases, are equivalent to or supersede what can be done in face-to-face classrooms. In any case, the most important consideration is that all assignments are designed to assess whether students have met desired instructional goals.

What constitutes an effective assessment, then, will vary from discipline to discipline. I do not have the content expertise to offer examples of exemplary online assessments in every K–12 content area. The purpose of this chapter, rather, is to provide general guidelines for effective online assessments, regardless of content.

HOW TO MAXIMIZE THE POWER OF THE INTERNET

One misconception of online learning, and educational technology in general, is the idea that simply because students are on the Internet, they are involved in engaging, constructivist instruction. Consider, for example, the webquest. An educational technology staple, webquests have become almost ubiquitous within educational circles, but very few webquests actually live up to the intended goal of fostering critical inquiry (Tally, 2007).

Most webquests, both in online and face-to-face classrooms, involve giving students a set of questions and telling them to find the answers on the Internet. How is this type of activity promoting critical inquiry? Other than teaching students how to use Google, this "webquest" is no different from having students define the boldfaced words at the end of a textbook chapter.

It is important for teachers to realize that just because students have access to untold amounts of information, simply accessing information does not equate to positive learning experiences. Regardless of the content area, true learning requires *engagement* with content.

TIPS FOR CREATING RELIABLE AND ACCESSIBLE ASSESSMENTS

Students Must Be Able to Open All Documents

There is nothing more frustrating for a teacher than creating a great activity only to find that half of his or her class cannot open the documents needed to complete it. Unless the school or district provides students with laptops that have software already installed, teachers are relying on the technology students have at home. If the computers that students use outside of school have outdated versions of Microsoft Word or PowerPoint, the students will not be able to read files produced with more recent versions.

An Example of an Engaging Webquest

Readers can access a webquest that I created for a ninth grade world history classroom here: http://www.uncg.edu/~awjourne/webquest. In this webquest, which focuses on the Middle Ages, students take the role of a knight and are charged with building a trebuchet, a type of catapult that is used to topple castle walls. The instructional goal of this activity is to show students that even in this era of history commonly known as the "Dark Ages" due to a lack of written records there was a demand for scientific innovation.

In this webquest, students are taken to several different websites: one that shows a picture of a trebuchet, one that explains why trebuchets were used, and one that diagrams the physics behind how a trebuchet works. Then, students are taken to a website where they play a game that simulates the firing of a trebuchet. In this game, students use the physics lessons they learned to find the correct settings that will allow them to destroy their enemy's castle. To conclude the webquest, students watch a video of President Reagan's address after the *Challenger* explosion and write an essay comparing scientific advancement and sacrifice over time.

Doesn't that activity sound more exciting than simply reading notes about knights in the Middle Ages and then filling in blanks on a worksheet? Online learning can be many things, but one thing it should never be is boring. Teachers often lament about all of the innovative things they would do in their classes if they could just get access to the computer lab on a daily basis. Online learning provides teachers with that opportunity.

Figure 3.1. An Example of an Engaging Webquest

Aside from creating frustration for students, technical glitches also give them a great excuse to avoid doing work or for submitting assignments late. Teachers can minimize those opportunities with a few basic steps. First, if teachers intend for a document to simply be read, it is best to convert it to a portable document format (PDF) and provide students with the link to a free download of Adobe Acrobat Reader (http://get.adobe.com/reader/).

All Word documents, PowerPoint presentations, and pictures can be converted to PDF files. Most Windows-based programs allow teachers to convert files to PDFs at the click of a button, but if teachers do not have that capability, they can download free software that will do the trick. One application that I have used before can be accessed at http://sourceforge.net/projects/pdfcreator/.

If, however, teachers intend for students to be able to enter data on a document (e.g., a Word document), it is best if they save documents into the most user-friendly format possible. At the most basic level is a text file (.txt), but one often loses a considerable amount of formatting with this option. A better choice would be to save Word documents as rich text format (RTF) files. An RTF file can be opened by any type of word processing program, as opposed to various versions of Microsoft Word (e.g., .doc or .docx) files or WordPerfect files, which can be opened using only that particular software.

It may go without saying, but the same rules apply to the files that students send to their teachers. After all, one cannot grade what one cannot open! Teachers should be specific on the types of files they will accept from students. As with files posted by teachers, most problems can be solved by having students submit assignments in RTF or PDF formats.

PowerPoint files are a little more complicated. Older versions of PowerPoint save files using the extension .ppt, and newer versions save using the extension .pptx. A PPT file can be opened with any version of PowerPoint, but a PPTX file cannot be opened in older versions of PowerPoint. Therefore, teachers should save all PowerPoint presentations as PPT files or post multiple versions to accommodate all students. (Note: This same issue exists with Microsoft Excel's XLS and XLSX file formats.)

A problem exists when students do not have PowerPoint or Excel on their computers. These files can easily be converted into PDF files, but they will lose any animation features as well as their ability to be manipulated. Yet students will still be able to see the content, so if that is the primary function of the file, converting to a PDF format is an adequate alternative.

Links Must Be Active and Tested

It stands to reason that online courses will make use of hyperlinks to websites. The key, though, is that teachers control where students go online rather than leaving it up to students to find information on their own. An assignment asking students to research a topic online may seem harmless, but teachers have to remember that although most adolescents are familiar with the Internet as a social tool, they are not necessarily adept at using it for academic purposes.

Here is a somewhat antiquated example of how leaving students to police themselves online can be a poor decision. Let's say that a government teacher asks his students to research the history of the White House as part of a unit on the executive branch. High school students who are not particularly Internet savvy may assume that the website address for the White House is www.whitehouse.com. If so, they will not find much to help them with their report; instead, they will stumble onto a politically themed pornographic website.[1]

Since most websites end with ".com," one can see how this would be a reasonable mistake that students could make. It is only after some experience dealing with government websites that one instinctively would identify the real White House website address as www.whitehouse.gov. The point is that it is less likely for students to stumble onto an inappropriate website if teachers provide them with links rather than sending them searching the Internet on their own. The last thing that any K–12 online teacher wants to see is an e-mail from an administrator asking why she just received a call from an irate parent who caught his or her child on a pornographic site that the child claimed was "part of his online class."

Another issue with hyperlinks that teachers often fail to consider is how they are structured to open once they are clicked. Most LMS systems provide options for hyperlinks to be "opened in another window." Teachers should always check that option. Most people have been in the situation where they have accidentally closed an Internet browser and lost everything they had been working on. Losing everything is frustrating for everyone, but for adolescents who may have procrastinated or lack motivation, it provides an excuse to not turn in work. Opening hyperlinks in a new window minimizes this excuse for students.

How to Effectively Convert Face-to-Face Lecture Notes Online

Lecture notes and other aspects of face-to-face lessons cannot just be uploaded to an LMS without modification. Teachers must take steps to include the stories and examples that they use to supplement their classroom lectures when putting these materials online. Otherwise, students will be left to make sense out of a skeleton set of notes that do not logically flow from one topic to another.

One option for teachers would be to write out all of this supplementary material. Online courses are already so heavy on text, however, that chances are students, especially auditory learners and poor readers, will either skim or completely ignore any additional material. A better option would be to create a podcast that could accompany lecture notes.

A podcast is nothing more than an audio file (usually in an MP3 format) that students can listen to on their computer or download to an iPod or other mobile device. Creating a podcast is simple; all one needs is a microphone and free software applications that can be downloaded online. A reliable application is Audacity (http://audacity.sourceforge.net/), but there are others that will work as well. Audacity is very simple to use; just click "record" and start speaking into the microphone.

The file that Audacity produces is a waveform audio (WAV) file. This type of file can be heard on students' computers through software applications such as Windows Media Player, but it will not work on most iPods or MP3 players. To convert a WAV file to an MP3 file, one simply needs a converter (googling "WAV to MP3 Converter" will display an array of free options). Once the file is in an MP3 format, students can download it to their iPod and listen to it at the gym or as they are driving across town, adding another element to "anytime, anywhere" learning. For a screencast on how to create a podcast using Audacity, refer to http://www.youtube.com/watch?v=CGykOAocS0o.

Here are a few final considerations when moving lecture notes online:

- Try to limit reading whenever possible. Especially for poor readers and English language learners, the more text based a course becomes, the less likely such students are to be successful.
- Make sure all material is written in a 12-point font or larger.
- Limit distractions to learning. Avoid sounds and extensive animations in PowerPoint presentations (Clark & Mayer, 2008).

Using Video in Online Courses

Videos can be an effective tool for online instruction. They break up the monotony of text, and they cater to both audio and visual learners. Teacher-made videos can also provide opportunities to replicate aspects of classroom instruction.

Consider, for example, a science teacher whose face-to-face instruction involves dissecting a fetal pig, a high school biology staple. This type of activity would be almost impossible to require of online students, but the teacher could make a video that demonstrates the dissection for students. It may not be as effective as having students perform the dissection themselves, but they could still see the process and be able to identify all of the required anatomical parts.

Making a video is relatively simple. All one needs is a webcam, microphone, and free software from the Internet. As with screencasts, there are several applications from which to choose, but I prefer Jing because of its compatibility with both Macs and PCs. Using this software, teachers can create a video that they can post on an LMS or on YouTube for students to watch.

YouTube also contains an untold amount of materials for online teachers. However, if students are completing their assignments in a location that regulates Internet use, such as a school computer lab, YouTube is often blocked. There is an easy way for teachers to get around this issue by downloading YouTube videos so that the Internet is not needed to play them.

Teachers should first find the YouTube video that they wish to use and then type the word "kiss" in front of the "youtube" part of the URL and press Enter. In other words, if the YouTube address is http://www.youtube/Sz54SX43L, then you would type http://www.kissyoutube/Sz54SX43L. Then, simply press Enter.

At that point, the website allows users to download the video in several different formats, usually a Flash video file (.flv) or a Media Player 4 file (.mp4). Unfortunately, few computers can play these files on their own. After downloading one of these files to their computer, teachers can then use free video conversion software (e.g., Any Video Converter, which can be downloaded at http://www.any-video-converter.com/products/for_video_free/) to convert it to other formats.

Most PCs will play Motion Picture Experts Group files (MPEG files) but may have difficulty with Mac-based applications, such as Quicktime/Audio Video Interleave (AVI) files, and vice versa. Therefore, I would recommend that teachers upload videos in multiple formats. To see a screencast of this process, refer to http://www.youtube.com/watch?v=aCbyAq4LHoM.

Implementing Group Work Online

Group work, admittedly, is more challenging online than in face-to-face classrooms. However, recent technologies have made online student collaborations much easier. Synchronous classrooms, such as Blackboard Collaborate, offer teachers the ability to put students into breakout rooms and have them brainstorm and work on tasks in groups. The Google+ hangout feature offers a free alternative to synchronous classroom technology, but it is limited in the number of users who can participate at one time.

Even if districts do not purchase synchronous classroom applications, there are other options for teachers who wish to engage their students in collaborative projects. Google Docs, for example, allows students to work together from a distance. Google Docs works similar to the whiteboard in Blackboard Collaborate in that whatever is written on the document can be seen by everyone with whom the document is shared. Students, therefore, could coordinate schedules and use Google Docs in a close-to-synchronous fashion to complete an assignment or simply use it as a way of staying abreast of what others have contributed to a larger group project.

CREATING A COURSE CALENDAR FOR ASSIGNMENTS

A point of contention in online courses is how to space out course requirements. Some instructors truly embrace the "anytime, anywhere" aspect of online learning and tell students to complete all of the course assignments by a specific date at the end of the semester. This may work for graduate students or adult learners, but it is a poor strategy for adolescents. Given that many adolescent online learners are already going to struggle with finding the intrinsic motivation needed to be successful, allowing them to procrastinate will only exacerbate that problem.

When teachers give students two weeks to complete a project in a face-to-face class, even the most idealistic teacher will admit that the average teenager will wait until a day or two before it is due to start *thinking* about it. The same theory holds true for adolescents in virtual classes. What may seem like a nice way to provide students with more autonomy over their learning is really only giving them license to complete an entire curriculum in a few days. More often than not, the result will be a failing grade.

For adolescents in online environments, a consistent schedule is a necessity for success. Teachers should require assignments to be submitted in regular intervals whenever possible. Again, forcing students to adhere to a schedule is similar to a classroom management technique in that it helps "train" students to get into a routine. For example, let's say that a teacher gives her students a week to complete a unit containing the recommended components outlined in the previous chapter. A sample schedule could look like this:

- *Monday*: Students complete and submit their activating prior knowledge assignment.
- *Tuesday*: Nothing is turned in; students should be reading and making an initial post on the discussion board.
- *Wednesday*: Students begin work on their individual and/or group assignments that show understanding of the material. Students also reply to classmates' posts on the discussion board. Some students will "meet" individually with the teacher to check progress.
- *Thursday*: Students continue to work on their individual and/or group assignments and reply to ongoing conversations on the discussion board. Those who did not "meet" individually with the teacher on Wednesday will meet to check progress.

- *Friday*: Students submit all individual and/or group assignments, including the reflection assignment, and attend the culminating synchronous session for the unit.

This is only a theoretical example of how a K–12 online course could be structured. If students follow a similar pattern throughout the course, it will eventually become routine.

Besides providing structure for students, there are other pedagogical justifications for establishing a regular schedule. Asynchronous communication becomes much more vibrant when students are given a schedule for posting on the discussion board. Also, setting a schedule for students means that teachers can settle into a routine themselves, which keeps procedural tasks, such as grading, manageable (Conceição & Lehman, 2011).

EFFECTIVE ONLINE ASSESSMENTS

The basic principles of assessment are the same online as in face-to-face classes, but the implementation is different (Rovai, 2000b). Teachers should strive to ensure that their assessments are reliable and accurate measures of their learning objectives. When it comes to deciding which type of assessments to use, online teachers have two basic options: summative or authentic. Each has pedagogical benefits and limitations; therefore, it is probably good practice to use a combination of both.

Summative Assessments

Summative assessments contain questions that can be graded objectively as either correct or incorrect. Multiple-choice, matching, and true-false tests or quizzes are examples of summative assessments. Although many students struggle with summative assessments, it is important for K–12 teachers to incorporate summative assessments into their courses.

Since most states' end-of-course assessments are entirely multiple choice, students must have adequate practice taking these types of assessments in order to be successful on the state test. There are other perks to summative assessments as well. For example, they are easy to grade (most LMSs have programs that will automatically grade summative assessments for teachers), and normally, they allow for fairly reliable comparisons among students.

The reliability of summative assessments comes into question, however, in online courses. The nature of online learning creates an environment that invites academic dishonesty. Unless assessments are proctored, there is no way for teachers to be sure that tests are being taken without the aid of outside materials or even by the student enrolled in the course.

For summative assessments to be reliable, then, they must be proctored (Bassoppo-Moyo, 2006; Rovai, 2000b). Teachers can require that students meet at an agreed-on location to take summative assessments, or they can require that students take them at established testing centers, such as Sylvan, which will proctor students for a fee. Either option restricts the "anytime, anywhere" element of online learning, however.

Another way in which online teachers can use summative assessments is to accept the reliability limitations and use them as learning tools. For example, teachers can make all of their summative assessments "open book" and institute a time limit.[2] This way, students can consult outside materials for the answers they do not know, which will hopefully aid in their learning of the material, but they will not have time to look up every answer.

Another option is to structure each assessment so that it is able to be taken multiple times without penalty. This approach requires that students make a perfect score before they are able to move on to the next unit. Making students take and retake assessments until they have shown mastery of the material can be an effective way to prepare students for end-of-course state assessments.

Authentic Assessments

Authentic assessments, on the other hand, are tasks that require students to create items that show mastery of learning objectives. These types of assessments are more subjective and rarely can be graded as simply correct or incorrect. Essays, projects, and discussion board posts are examples of authentic assessments. Although it is possible for a student to have someone else complete the course assignments, authentic assessments are generally more challenging to fake and, therefore, fairly reliable. I would recommend that the vast majority of assignments in online courses be authentic assessments.

Authentic assessments are harder to grade than summative assessments. Given that most authentic assessments will display varying degrees of correctness, it is a good idea for teachers to use rubrics to maintain consistency.[3] Assessing student comments in threaded discussion boards is especially tricky and requires teachers to make decisions regarding quantity versus quality of student participation. Most other types of assignments, however, will follow similar procedures as in face-to-face classes.

TIPS FOR STAYING ORGANIZED WHILE GRADING

Beyond general assessment guidelines, there are a few logistical aspects of grading and providing feedback to students that are unique to online learning (Quinlan, 2011). Take, for example, the turning in of student work. On the day an assignment is due, teachers will receive a large number of electronic files, and it can be difficult to keep these files organized.

Unless students put their name on their work (which, as most teachers know, is far from guaranteed), it is easy to transpose files, especially if they are all named some variation of "Unit 3 Webquest." This type of confusion can cause teachers to spend valuable time opening files from old e-mails to correctly match students with their work. Although this problem sounds fairly simple to fix, one can imagine the amount of time that could be wasted in a class of 25 students.

A helpful trick is to explicitly state how students should name their files. One option would be to have students use their last name as the first part of the name of any file they submit. Then, the remainder of the file name should identify the specific assignment. For example, if Michelle Andrews turned in the webquest from Unit 3, her file would be named something like "andrews3webquest." The actual naming protocol is up to the teacher; the key is to be consistent and explicit. It will save a lot of time throughout the span of a course.

Another tip that teachers can convey to their students is the value of saving files in multiple locations. Losing work due to a computer or thumb drive crashing is frustrating for anyone, but many adolescents will use it as an excuse to turn in assignments late or avoid doing the work at all. A great tool that can help teachers and students stay organized is a free Dropbox (www.dropbox.com) account, which allows users to protect their work by saving it to the Dropbox server.

PROVIDING FEEDBACK ONLINE

Providing feedback to students is an essential part of the learning process. However, it can be tedious online. Teachers will find that many students will make the same mistakes on a particular assignment, and sending e-mails to 20 students saying roughly the same thing makes for a long grading process. A trick that will save time is sending an e-mail that outlines any widespread issues to the entire class after grading an assignment. Then, teachers can spend their time focusing on specific students who may have had more trouble with the assignment.

Teachers should also make use of technology when providing feedback. Long, detailed e-mails back to students are nice, but they can be challenging for students who struggle with reading. Using the track changes and comments features of Microsoft Word, for example, can help teachers pinpoint specific issues for students.

Typing comments can be tedious, however, and as a result, teachers may not go into as much detail as they would if they were discussing the assignment with the student face-to-face. A way to simulate this experience is to use the screencast video software. Teachers can open the assignment on their screen and then verbally discuss any issues that may exist as they scroll through the document. This approach is especially beneficial for auditory learners and students who struggle with reading.

SUMMARY

Assignments in online courses should use technology to engage students with content as opposed to masking low-level tasks that are designed to encourage rote memorization of facts. When creating assignments, teachers should bear in mind the following aspects:

- Document files should be in the least restrictive format possible to ensure students can open them.
- Links should be checked for accuracy and should open in new windows.
- Lecture notes should be condensed whenever possible and should include audio options for auditory learners and poor readers.

Also, teachers should establish a routine for students with respect to assignment submission. A consistent course calendar provides students with structure and will help ensure completion of work. Finally, quality feedback is essential to any type of learning environment, and online teachers must take steps to ensure that their feedback meets the needs of all learners.

NOTES

1. This is actually a true story. When I first started teaching, the website www.whitehouse.com was a politically themed pornographic site. It has since been changed to a site that more accurately reflects its URL address.

2. Most LMSs have security options for summative assessments that allow teachers to shut down an assessment after a predetermined period of time and prohibit students from exiting an assessment once they have started it. One pitfall to these features is that if students lose Internet access during an assessment, the LMS will lock the assessment, and the teacher will have to manually reopen it for the student.

3. Although consistency in grading is generally ideal, another advantage to authentic assessments is that they allow teachers to differentiate grading policies for certain students, such as students with learning disabilities or English language learners. For a detailed discussion on the merits of using rubrics as a method of differentiation, see McLaughlin & Lewis, 2004 and Whittaker, Salend, & Duhaney, 2001.

Chapter Four

Building Community in Online Courses

When online learning first emerged in higher education, many critics were quick to question the social aspect of self-directed learning. As most educators attest, the benefits of schooling extend beyond simply acquiring content. The indirect lessons students glean from interacting in classroom environments with others, or what is commonly referred to as the "hidden curriculum" (Giroux & Purpel, 1983), are valuable to their social and emotional development.

Even today, many of those unfamiliar with online learning still conjure images of students hunched over a keyboard, scrolling through websites and writing papers with few opportunities for collaboration with others. Research, however, has shown that online students crave social interaction, and when given the opportunity, a sense of community can be developed among students even in the absence of physical proximity (e.g., Haythornthwaite & Kazmer, 2004; Rovai, 2001). Although most of the research in this area has been conducted within a higher education context, much of it can be applied to K–12 online learning.

In particular, scholars have found that building and sustaining community in online courses requires three criteria:

- A belief among teachers and students that interaction is valuable to online learning
- Regular opportunities for interaction (preferably both synchronous and asynchronous)
- Targeted efforts to both increase students' social presence and decrease feelings of distance

This chapter will discuss the importance of creating the expectation for social interaction online by looking at a case in which neither the teacher nor his students seemed to believe interaction was necessary to academic success. Then I will discuss strategies teachers can use to build social presence and encourage communication both among students and between themselves and their students.

TEACHER AND STUDENT PERCEPTIONS OF SOCIAL INTERACTION ONLINE

Perhaps the most important factor in shaping a sense of community online is whether the participants feel social interaction is necessary. If teachers and students perceive online learning as merely content transformation, then it is likely that few opportunities for student collaboration will be given, and students will not see the pedagogical benefit of the opportunities that do exist. This attitude is more likely to exist among individuals who are inexperienced with online instruction, making this an issue for K–12 districts seeking to establish online learning programs.

The Importance of Teacher Perceptions

To illustrate this point, I will share data that I collected several years ago from a case study of an online K–12 U.S. history class. The teacher, Mr. Harding, had little experience with online learning prior to being asked by the district to create and teach the online U.S. history course. Like many K–12 online teachers, Mr. Harding was chosen because he was considered an excellent classroom teacher with a solid grasp of content. Mr. Harding also received little training from the district in online pedagogy prior to teaching his first online class.

When I asked Mr. Harding to describe his teaching philosophy, he made a point of distinguishing between ways of helping students academically versus socially and proceeded to argue that online learning catered to only the former goal. Here is his response:

> Now the goal may be academic; that is what it is obviously, almost exclusively online. It's an academic goal, as in pass the [end-of-course] test, learning the information at a level well enough to, you know, demonstrate to the state that you actually know American history.

Mr. Harding then compared online learning to classroom instruction by saying,

> In the classroom you obviously add in the social component, and the goal is going to be to obviously exceed well beyond the academic goal. The goal there would be, in the classroom, to help the students develop themselves socially, to become confident in themselves, to enjoy the day.

I then asked Mr. Harding which of these goals, social or academic, was more important to his views of education, and we had the following conversation:

Wayne: Now do you think one [of these goals] is better than the other?

Mr. Harding: Yeah, I'd say in the classroom is a better goal.

Wayne: Why?

Mr. Harding: Because I think that most students, including myself, will forget the vast majority of information that you learn in the classroom, the rote memorization, which means ultimately, maybe you have a short-term goal that is accomplished or achieved, but for the long term, academics are largely meaningless.

I don't think the vast majority of my students are going to remember, I don't know, pick out a battle—the Battle of Antietam, let's say—10 years from now. Not a big deal, you know?

Now I understand academically, they are learning a variety of things, like you know, memorization and time management and all of those sort of things, but I think that academically the short-term goals of, that illustrate that they have learned X amount of information is largely worthless in the long term. Socially, on the other hand, if they can become confident in themselves, if they can ascertain where their strengths and weaknesses are, if they will socially come out in the classroom and interact with others in a productive way, then that, to me, far exceeds the value of academics.

Wayne: And do you think they do that in the online course?

Mr. Harding: No.

Wayne: What do you think their goal is online?

Mr. Harding: I think their goal is to pass the [end-of-course test]. Get in, get out of it, minimize your interaction or input.

As this conversation shows, Mr. Harding valued social interaction in his classroom, but not in his online course. Based on his comments, Mr. Harding seemed to perceive online learning as primarily a medium for transmitting content to students, one that paled in comparison to classroom instruction and that did not provide the necessary social and emotional aspects he believed were essential to an engaging learning experience.

Mr. Harding also seemed to connect his beliefs about online education to his characterization of online students. According to Mr. Harding, students took his online course because their "whole goal . . . is to put in the minimal amount [of effort] possible." As he quipped during our interview, "I mean, there is a reason why they are doing it online; they don't want to be in the classroom!" He then compared his online students to

> The students in the classroom among the bottom 10% that don't want to interact with me. You know the kids I am talking about. They come in, take their seats, they're quiet, they give you one-word answers, and they are out the door. I see them, but I don't interact with them much. That is kind of how it is online.

These opinions of his online students and the viability of online instruction to meet the same social aspects found in the classroom seemed to affect Mr. Harding's instructional choices online. He admitted that his online course involved more rote memorization and repetition of content than his classroom instruction. As he said,

> For the kid that simply wants to do the minimum, just give me the information, be quiet, spit it back to you and we're fine, then the online [course] is the better place because all I do with them is worksheets. Well not all I do, but one of the aspects is worksheets. We don't do any worksheets all year long in my regular (classroom) class. For the minimalist that just wants to crank in and get out, [online] is better.

As one can see, how a teacher perceives online instruction will shape the type of course he creates. Mr. Harding's views on the inadequacy of online instruction to meet the social needs of his students, which were never corrected through training, led to a course that offered no synchronous communication options and a loosely monitored asynchronous discussion board.

The Reality of Student Perceptions

Sadly, Mr. Harding's opinions of his online students were not completely inaccurate. Research on adolescent online learners suggests that many either fail to see the importance of social interaction or lack the intrinsic motivation to collaborate with peers unless specifically instructed to by their teachers (e.g., Herring & Clevenger-Schmertzing, 2007; Tunison & Noonan, 2001; Weiner, 2003). In that same study, I interviewed 11 of the 13 students enrolled in Mr. Harding's U.S. history course and found most to hold dismissive attitudes toward online learning as a viable option for engaged learning.

When I asked the students in his class why they decided to take U.S. history online, the majority of their responses centered on the perception that online learning offered a quicker and easier approach to learning than what they would have received in the classroom. As Walter said, "You get through [content] faster. You do a lot more in less time." Another student even boasted that "I am taking two [online] classes in like two months [over the summer] or something like that, and I get my whole junior year out of the way."

As with Mr. Harding, there seemed to be a perception among the students that online learning was the option for those simply trying to earn required credit and not wishing to engage in the material. As Cynthia, one of the top-performing students in the class, admitted, "[History] doesn't have anything to do with what I really want to go into, so that's also why I am doing it [online]."

Many students also seemed to believe that online courses were less rigorous than traditional classes. Although several students equated ease with flexibility, as was the case of Brandon, who described online learning as easier because "you don't have to actually get up and go to class. You can sit there and plan out your whole day with it," other students viewed online instruction as a way to easily learn large amounts of content. As Jennifer noted, "It would be a lot harder to take a math or science course [online], but history is a lot of facts and memorization."

This attitude also seemed to affect students' perceptions of the need for social interaction. Like Mr. Harding, most of his students did not perceive online learning as conducive to developing a sense of community. As Brandon stated,

> I haven't really gotten to know [his classmates] much because I haven't talked to them. It's just like the discussion boards, that's the only way you get to talk to them, and you're just debating about history so it's not like you really have a connection.

Similar student attitudes toward social interaction have been found in other research on K–12 online learning. For example, in a study of an online high school world history class, Herring and Clevenger-Schmertzing (2007) found that students rarely posted to the course discussion board unless it was required by their teacher, and even then, students often failed to respond to classmates' posts. These students also reported dissatisfaction with the teacher's attempts to create opportunities for synchronous class meetings.

Ironically, it was clear in my conversations with Mr. Harding's students that many seemed to crave the personal interaction that they had grown accustomed to in face-to-face classrooms. Several students even unfavorably compared the online course to their classroom experiences because of the missing social component in their online instruction. Responding to my question of whether he preferred taking classes online versus in the classroom, Jason replied, "Probably in the classroom due to more hands on [learning]; I like the atmosphere more than just sitting at your computer learning the material."

Bill answered the same question by saying, "Online you're kind of pulled out. The classroom is a little more fun." When I asked him why the classroom was more enjoyable, he said, "Because you can't really do group activities and talk with your friends and stuff. It's like with me, I get on Instant Messenger while I am taking the class; that way I can still talk to friends while I am doing it."

Students *can,* however, engage in group activities and communicate with each other online if their teachers provide adequate opportunities for social interaction. Based on my interviews with the students and other research on K–12 online education, it appears that teachers may need to be more forceful in their approach to fostering a sense of community with adolescents than they might with older students.

Regardless, it seems clear that the first step toward socially constructivist online learning is having teachers acknowledge that social interaction is both necessary and possible online. I do not include this data to vilify Mr. Harding; rather, it is intended to illustrate the ramifications of throwing a teacher into online instruction without proper training in online learning theory. Fortunately, teachers can improve the sense of community in their classes by implementing several simple strategies.

STRATEGIES FOR BUILDING CLASSROOM COMMUNITY

The structure of a course must reflect an expectation of social interaction. Opportunities for synchronous and asynchronous academic collaboration and discussion are obviously essential, but to truly develop a sense of community, teachers need to provide students with avenues for nonacademic social interaction as well. These noncurricular opportunities for interaction are designed to increase students' feelings of social presence, which is defined as the degree to which one is aware of others in their environment and feels part of an interpersonal relationship with them (Tu & McIsaac, 2002).

Increasing students' social presence also has academic implications. If students feel a part of a community, they are less likely to become "lurkers," which Rovai (2000a) defines as students who are essentially observers of course interactions who do not give anything back to the community. Lurkers can make students who participate nervous or self-conscious about what they are saying or posting because it might seem as though their ideas are constantly being judged.

A strong sense of social presence also lessens the chances of students feeling as though they are learning in isolation. Feelings of alienation in online classes have been linked to poor academic performance and student dropout rates (Rovai & Wighting, 2005). Students who feel as though they know their classmates and teachers are more likely to become engaged in academic conversations and seek help if they begin to struggle with assignments.

Here are a few easy strategies that all teachers can use in their courses to help strengthen students' social presence and build a sense of community:

Hold an Initial Face-to-Face Meeting

Research has shown that holding at least one face-to-face meeting prior to the start of an online class does wonders for building classroom community (Haythornthwaite, Kazmer, Robins, & Shoemaker, 2004). For most K–12 students who have limited experience with online learning, being able to meet their classmates and teacher in a familiar environment will decrease feelings of anxiety as well as strengthen feelings of social presence. A face-to-face meeting also provides teachers with an opportunity to clearly articulate course expectations and descriptions of major assignments.

The primary focus of the face-to-face meeting, however, should be community building. Similar to what might occur on the first day of a regular class, teachers should give students opportunities to tell something about themselves as well as learn information about their classmates. Icebreaker activities are a great way for students to informally share a little bit about themselves without putting shy students "on the spot."

It would be unrealistic to expect all students to be best friends at the end of this initial meeting. That is not the point. If students can make one or two meaningful connections during this initial meeting, those connections can be used as a starting point for interaction in the online course. One comment to a "friend" on a discussion board, for example, could lead to others responding to that comment, and before long a conversation has begun.

Have Students Introduce Themselves Online

In the cases where an initial face-to-face meeting is impossible due to geographical concerns or other logistical limitations, teachers should not give up on having students get to know each other. Online introductions can be effective, although additional steps are often necessary. Teachers should use a synchronous format for course introductions if possible. A system like Blackboard Collaborate would be very similar to a face-to-face meeting.

Students could talk to each other through microphones, and teachers could even put smaller groups of students in separate "rooms" to complete various icebreaker activities.

Asynchronous introductions will obviously require students to post written information about themselves for their classmates to read. On one hand, this approach allows students to provide detailed descriptions of themselves. On the other, students are less likely to spend the time necessary to read all of their classmates' posts. As one of Mr. Harding's students told me, "I don't really have a relationship with [others in the class] just because, you know, you can only see what they wrote about the class. The only personal thing that we did was the introduction, and I didn't read everybody's."

Posting introductions, therefore, cannot be an activity that is completed and then ignored. Teachers need to take steps to ensure that students are actually reading others' introductions. One strategy would be to put students in small groups within the discussion board and then have them respond to each other's introductions and identify common interests. Another idea might be for teachers to read students' introductions first and create items for a scavenger hunt (e.g., "Find someone who likes country music") that students have to complete as they read their classmates' posts. Regardless of the activity, the purpose should be to have students read as many of their classmates' posts as possible.

Have Students Post Pictures of Themselves

For many people who have trouble remembering names, being able to put a name with a face is essential. Encouraging students to post pictures of themselves alongside their personal introductions is another way in which teachers can help build social presence in their courses. Also, teachers could have their students create Google accounts, which allow for the posting of pictures as part of one's profile. Then, when students use Google for collaborative assignments (e.g., Google docs), they would be able to have a visual image of the individuals with whom they are working.

There are a couple of issues for teachers to consider, however, before having students post photographs online. First, students may be taking online courses because of the anonymity that online learning provides. Students of minority groups, those with physical disabilities, or others who may normally feel discriminated against in traditional face-to-face classrooms may not want to post photographs of themselves. An alternative requirement, then, is to give students the option of posting a photograph of themselves or an image that represents an aspect of their personality.

Another requirement should be that the photographs or images must be appropriate for a school setting. Students might be able to get a lot of attention with half-naked photographs of themselves, but that is not the type of community that teachers want to build in their courses. Students need to be cognizant of the academic setting they are in, especially if they use their personal accounts for collaborative assignments.

Create a "Coffee House" Area

A final way teachers can develop a sense of community in their courses is to designate a specific discussion board forum just for students. Within the literature, this type of space is often referred to as a "coffee house" in that the purpose is to let students socialize, share ideas, and ask each other questions about assignments. As a general rule, teachers will want to have access to the coffee house to ensure that all conversations are appropriate, but beyond that, it should be left to students to moderate.

As with the posting of personal introductions, teachers may want to provide a few incentives to get students into the coffee house. For example, teachers could give extra credit to the first student to pose a question or answer a classmate's post. Once students see the benefit of having their own space within the course, they will hopefully use it to its full potential.

FOSTERING RELATIONSHIPS BETWEEN TEACHERS AND STUDENTS

One of the more disconcerting findings from my study of Mr. Harding's class was the number of students who seemed to perceive Mr. Harding as unimportant to their learning of history. None of the students made any reference to Mr. Harding guiding their learning, and most stated that the only time they contacted him was to seek technology support or ask procedural questions related to missing work or scheduling concerns. As Jennifer said, "The only time I ever e-mailed him was when I noticed a mistake on my grades and he fixed it and apologized." In a similar comment, Pete said, "I have talked to him a couple times about the links not working and stuff."

In my conversations with these students, it seemed that most recognized this lack of academic communication and found it inferior to the relationships they had formed with teachers in a traditional classroom setting. As Jason stated, "I think maybe if there was a way to lessen that gap [between students and teachers], I think the online experience would be a little bit better."

Several students also attributed their poor relationship with Mr. Harding to the lack of physical presence one would typically find in a classroom. As Allen stated, "It's definitely different because you don't have the face-to-face. You don't know him as well, I guess." Pete continued by saying, "I mean, I wouldn't really consider us having a relationship because I don't really know him, but I mean, if you are in a classroom with a teacher day after day, you start to know him, you see him, you can kind of, like, relate to him."

This academic disconnect between students and their teacher contradicts most prominent educational theories (e.g., Vygotsky, 1978). It is widely accepted in educational circles that students must learn in the presence of experts who act as mentors and facilitators. These theories are just as relevant online. Just because students are learning at a distance does not mean that they are learning on their own.

The role of an online teacher does not end once a course is created. Online teachers are expected to monitor student learning, and just like in the classroom, this is made much easier when teachers develop working relationships with their students. The following strategies can be used to ensure that teachers do not simply become faceless graders of assignments in online courses.

Create a Welcome Video

The same process for creating instructional videos using a webcam can be used to create a welcome video for an online course. A welcome video becomes even more important if teachers are unable to hold an initial face-to-face meeting with their students. Absent a face-to-face meeting, a welcome video may be the best chance teachers have at making a first impression, and it allows students to put a name with a face.

Teachers will want to keep the welcome video short—it is not intended to be a lecture—and fairly light in nature. Besides welcoming students to the course, the video is an opportunity for teachers to tell a little about themselves and what students can expect in the class. One tip: In order to appear coherent in the video, teachers should not attempt to "wing it."

Instead, type out the welcome message and then tape it to the front of the computer screen. That way, as teachers read, it will appear as though they are looking into the camera as opposed to having students stare at a three-minute video of the top of their head. Teachers could then have students create introductory videos of themselves as a way to get to know their students.

Create Opportunities for Private Discussions with Students

Coffee houses and other types of forums where students can ask questions are great for informal conversations, but when students need to ask questions of their teachers, greater privacy is needed. Research has shown that there is a relationship between feelings of privacy in online courses and students' social presence (Tu, 2002), so providing opportunities for students to privately discuss academic concerns with their teachers is essential to academic success. A variety of methods are available to help teachers achieve this goal, and teachers should use several options in their courses.

The most obvious way in which teachers and students can communicate is via e-mail. The limitation of e-mail, however, is that it does not provide immediate feedback. Online teachers should be expected to check their e-mail regularly, but even the most attentive teachers cannot be at their computers all the time.

Instead, all teachers should keep regular virtual office hours. At a designated time, students would know that their teacher will be at his or her computer and available for immediate response via e-mail. This way, the e-mail feedback will be close to synchronous. An even better option, however, would be to offer students the option of contacting their teacher via an instant messenger program (e.g., Yahoo!, Google Chat, AOL Instant Messenger). Teachers could then answer questions in real time and juggle several student conversations at a time if necessary.

Office hours are often the loneliest hours a teacher will spend each week. Yet it is important that teachers at least offer the opportunity for students to contact their teachers for a real-time conversation. Teachers may be contacted during their office hours by only a handful of students throughout the span of a course, but for those students, being able to communicate directly with their teacher may reduce anxiety and feelings of alienation.

Other asynchronous options that are included in most LMSs are private wikis and blogs. These tools are not necessarily useful for addressing student concerns, but they are a great way to have private discussions of content with students. Students can post reflections about content on their blogs or wikis, and then their teachers can post responses afterward. In short, wikis and blogs allow for the in-depth individual engagement between teachers and students over content that is rarely replicated in other aspects of online courses (or face-to-face courses, for that matter).

One-on-One Videoconferences

A videoconference offers online teachers and students a chance to meet face to face. Free software, such as Skype or Google+ Hangouts, can be used to set up these meetings, and all that is needed is for both parties to have webcam and microphone capabilities. Unlike the office hours, teachers can mandate the use of videoconferencing as a way to maintain regular contact with students. Perhaps once a week teachers could require that students schedule video appointments to meet and discuss assignment feedback or any other concerns either party may have.

There are two obvious limitations to videoconferencing, however. First, the scheduling of appointments detracts from the "anytime, anywhere" benefit of online learning. The other limitation is that, unlike instant messenger programs, teachers can only videoconference with one student at a time, which raises additional scheduling concerns. Despite these limitations, however, videoconferencing remains a powerful way to lessen the distance between teachers and students and increase feelings of social presence in online courses.

SUMMARY

Building and sustaining a sense of community remains one of the more challenging aspects of teaching online. Research has shown that community can exist online, but only if teachers and students buy into the necessity of social interaction in self-directed learning. Online teachers can take the following steps to build community in their courses beyond requiring collaborative assignments:

- Hold initial face-to-face meetings.
- Have students introduce themselves online.
- Have students post pictures of themselves.
- Create a "coffee house" area.

Implementing opportunities for nonacademic social interaction is essential to students' academic success as research has shown it to strengthen students' feelings of social presence and lessen feelings of alienation in online courses.

Many of these same principles also apply to the relationships teachers establish with their students. Teachers can take the following steps to foster more personal relationships with their online students:

- Create a welcome video.
- Hold virtual office hours.
- Create opportunities for private academic dialogue between teachers and students.
- Mandate regular one-on-one videoconferencing.

For students, regular contact with their teachers increases feelings of social presence, and teachers can use these interactions to monitor student progress and engage students in discussions of content.

NOTE

The data included in this chapter were taken from two of my previously published articles: The first, from 2008, is "Facilitating Historical Discussions Using Asynchronous Communication: The Role of the Teacher," which appeared in *Theory and Research in Social Education*, *36*, pp. 317–355. The second, from 2010, is "Perceptions of E-Learning in Secondary Education: A

Viable Alternative to Classroom Instruction or a Way to Bypass Engaged Learning?" and was published in *Educational Media International, 47*, pp. 69–81.

Chapter Five

Creating Substantive Asynchronous Discussions

Research has shown that most K–12 online courses make greater use of asynchronous forms of communication than synchronous discussions (e.g., Murphy et al., 2011). Yet studies of online learning have found that teachers view monitoring asynchronous discussions more challenging than synchronous chats and tend to assign less substantive work to be discussed asynchronously. Students, perhaps as a result, often find asynchronous discussions less meaningful than synchronous communication (e.g., Barbour, 2007, 2008).

Unlike synchronous chats, which operate in a way similar to face-to-face conversations, asynchronous discussions are unfamiliar to novice online teachers and students. Therefore, simply creating discussion board threads, posing questions, and telling students to interact with each other will most likely not lead to the type of substantive engagement needed to sustain a social constructivist learning environment. In this chapter, I return to Mr. Harding's U.S. history course for an example of the problems that can occur when asynchronous discussion boards are left unstructured and virtually unmonitored. I will then offer recommendations for facilitating engaging asynchronous discussions based on these findings.

A CASE STUDY OF ASYNCHRONOUS COMMUNICATION IN A K–12 ONLINE COURSE

Brief Description of Methodology

Nearly all of the units in Mr. Harding's course contained an asynchronous discussion component.[1] Participation in the discussion board was required, although no clear guidelines for an appropriate level of participation were given on the course syllabus or in the face-to-face meeting prior to the start of the course. The weight of the discussion board grade was usually 10% of each unit grade.

In this case study, I analyzed all of the discussion board postings throughout the course of the semester. At the conclusion of each unit, I analyzed the hierarchy of each discussion thread and noted the number of original posts and replies made by Mr. Harding and each of his students. I then printed each of the individual posts for coding purposes.

I then conducted a content analysis of the statements contained in each individual post in order to determine whether the statement substantively promoted authentic historical discussion. In cases of missing or erratic punctuation, I considered indications of new thoughts as individual statements. After determining whether statements were substantive or nonsubstantive, I then created subcategories to further delineate the statements. The following sections illustrate what I found after analyzing the content from the course discussion board.

FACTORS LEADING TO UNPRODUCTIVE DISCUSSIONS

Unequal Participation

One issue that seemed to affect the quality of historical discussions during the course was unequal participation with regard to number and detail of student posts. Table 5.1 highlights the difference in the number of total posts, replies to classmates, and total statements made by participants throughout the span of the course.

Four students, Cynthia, Jennifer, Allen, and Brandon, appeared to carry the conversation in terms of both quantity and substance. Walter and Amy made up a second tier of participation; both students made considerably fewer posts than the four previously mentioned students, but the total number of statements in their posts suggests that they took care to produce lengthy responses. The rest of the class minimally interacted on the discussion board, and when they did, their responses were often brief.

Table 5.1. Student and Teacher Discussion Board Participation

	Total Number of Posts	Number of Replies	Total Number of Statements
Amy	19	8	126
Beth	2	0	26
Cynthia	46	35	370
Jennifer	35	29	219
Nicole	10	6	69
Rebecca	5	1	34
Allen	38	27	156
Bill	11	1	55
Brandon	32	21	232
Hunter	14	4	73
Jason	14	3	85
Pete	13	4	53
Walter	18	7	155
Mr. Harding	17	16	41
TOTAL	274	162	1,694

These differences can be seen in the quality of individual posts as well. Consider, for example, Hunter's response to a prompt questioning American involvement in World War I[2]:

> I think the U.S. did the right thing being aggressive. If they would not have done what they did the U.S. probably would not have grown to be so strong. I believe that they did the right thing when they sent troops to Europe. I believe that sooner or later we would have been in World War I and I think that we saved ourselves a lot of threats to our country by going in. The power of the U.S. army would have not been with the Allies. I just think that we would have suffered big time if we went into the war any later.

Then, compare his response with a mere excerpt from Cynthia's response to the same question:

> Then with WWI the US first off did try to stay out of the war with Wilson's declaration of neutrality but when their old comrades in Britain and England were being attacked it made it very hard. After all, despite the fact that the US had separated themselves from England and Great Britain many years earlier, the US's connection with them was still very strong because in addition to their long history/ancestry the US also had very strong cultural and economic ties with both Great Britain and England making the US want to help out their

old allies in any way they could. Another big factor, probably the most important, was the fact that American ships were getting attacked by Germany, who may were just trying to keep the US out of the war, but they had a horrible way of doing it because how can any nation that is supposed to protect its people just sit back and let something like the purposeful sinking of the Lusitania, which killed over 1,000 people may I add, go unnoticed? They can't! The US had to take up some kind of defense against this sort of action and besides when the US was actually being singled out it no longer made the war and even the people were behind the nation joining the war.

Despite Cynthia's apparent confusion over Great Britain and England being the same nation, one can see how her post provides a more convincing historical argument than Hunter's. While Hunter does hint at German aggression prior to American intervention into World War I, Cynthia focuses on submarine attacks and lists the famous example of the *Lusitania*.

Cynthia also expresses her opinion on U.S. involvement in World War I through an analysis of the relationship between the United States and Britain. Cynthia also frames her post around a rationale that a nation must protect its citizens, even if that means going to war. Hunter chooses to personalize his opinions without providing sufficient evidence to support his claims, instead using vague terms such as "suffering big time" to justify his position.

The student interaction on the discussion board also lacked depth in terms of students replying to one another. Outside of the slavery unit, the course discussion boards contained only one tertiary response, meaning that the original poster revisited the discussion board and responded to comments regarding his or her original post. This one instance occurred between Cynthia and Mr. Harding during the Reconstruction unit, when Mr. Harding asked for clarification regarding Cynthia's opinion on the impact of Lincoln's assassination.

Nine of the eleven students I interviewed stated that they did go back to the discussion board to see whether others replied to their posts at the completion of each unit. Yet the majority of students seemed disinterested in continuing conversations with others. Without being expressly required by Mr. Harding to revisit the discussion board to carry on conversations, students chose to let conversations die.

Lack of Substantive Conversations

As part of the study, I conducted a content analysis in which I coded each statement made by students or Mr. Harding on the discussion board as either substantive or nonsubstantive. I considered substantive statements those that used historical evidence, actively agreed with others' posts, posed questions to others, directly responded to questions posed by others, or disagreed with or challenged others' beliefs. I labeled statements as nonsubstantive that expressed unsubstantiated opinions, offered simple encouragement, passively agreed with others' posts, or provided recreational banter.

Table 5.2 provides examples of statements that would fall within each category.

Table 5.2. Coding Scheme for Discussion Board Posts

Substantive Statements		
Use of historical evidence (HE)	Statements that support claims with evidence learned in the course	Ex: The South lost the Civil War because of their lack of supplies, eventually resorting to throwing rocks at Union soldiers.
Active agreement (AA)	Statements that agree with others and explain why or offer clarification	Ex: I agree that Lincoln helped the Union win; the Emancipation Proclamation helped turn the tide of the war.
Posing a question to others (PQ)	Statements that ask for clarification or opinions from others	Ex: Why do you think dropping the atomic bombs saved lives?
Responses to questions (RQ)	Statements that directly responded to questions from others	Ex: Yes, I think Lincoln's assassination hurt Reconstruction.
Disagreement/challenge beliefs (D)	Statements that either disagreed or challenged others' beliefs	Ex: I disagree that slavery was the cause of the Civil War; the agriculture of the South forced them to have slaves.
Nonsubstantive Statements		
Unsubstantiated opinions (UO)	Statements that expressed opinions without any historical evidence	Ex: I believe WWII was the most important event of the century.
Encouraging remarks (ER)	Statements intended to motivate	Ex: Good job, Cynthia!
Passive agreement (PA)	Statements that agree with others without clarifying why	Ex: I agree with everything you said.
Recreational (R)	Statements that are off topic	Ex: Sorry my post was so long!

Even when students did participate in the discussion board, their attempts at engaging in historical dialogue often lacked substance. The coding of individual posts found that nonsubstantive statements were used more often than substantive statements, and students relied predominantly on unsubstantiated opinions to support their positions.

Table 5.3 lists the coding results for each individual.[3]

Table 5.3. Total Number of Substantive and Nonsubstantive Statements Made by Participants

	Nonsubstantive				Substantive			
	UO	ER	PA	R	AA	PQ	D	HE
Amy	72	0	3	0	1	1	8	41
Beth	5	0	0	0	0	0	0	21
Cynthia	169	0	32	3	11	3	11	140
Jennifer	115	1	22	1	10	1	6	63
Nicole	28	1	5	0	5	0	1	29
Rebecca	24	0	0	0	0	1	0	9
Allen	57	1	23	7	3	2	13	50
Bill	40	0	5	1	0	1	0	8
Brandon	86	1	29	0	7	8	7	94
Hunter	52	0	0	0	0	1	2	18
Jason	51	0	2	0	1	1	3	27
Pete	31	0	1	0	1	2	1	17
Walter	98	0	7	0	4	0	6	40
Mr. Harding	1	18	1	1	2	12	1	5
TOTAL	829	22	130	13	45	33	59	562
	Total nonsubstantive: 994				Total substantive: 700			

Perhaps most disturbing from a social constructivist standpoint is the lack of disagreement or challenging of beliefs that leads to multiple perspectives of history. The dialogue that occurred in the discussion board appeared to center on passively agreeing with others' responses and ignoring new ideas or calls for clarification.

The following thread from the Jacksonian unit is indicative of the type of interaction found throughout the course. Students were asked to place themselves in President Jackson's shoes and give their opinion on how best to regulate westward expansion:

> *Jennifer:* I would try to make a deal with the Indians and Mexicans. Let them live where they want and let Americans live in the other places, or see if they could live together peacefully. After all, if you prohibit people from moving west, they would think that it was too much like the British Government that they fought to get away from. And, it is inhumane to force Indians and Mexicans from their homelands, where they have lived

for centuries. As president, I would set up punishments for anyone who were cruel to the natives. It would not be a good idea to stop Americans from westward expansion, because otherwise the East would become overpopulated, and there would not be many economic opportunities for the citizens. I would just try to limit the amount of people who did move west, and set up settlements where they could live and not disturb the Indians.

Allen (to Jennifer): I agree that you should try to make a deal with them, or try to live peacefully with them, and that it's inhumane to try and force them out of their homeland.

Brandon (to Jennifer): I agree with what you are saying. I would try to help the Indians and Mexicans without making them move out of their homelands. I think that is wrong. As President I would have done exactly what you are thinking.

Walter (to Jennifer): I agree. I especially thought you made a good point when you pointed out that the East would be overpopulated. I also agree with your statement "I would just try to limit the amount of people who did move west, and set up settlements where they could live and not disturb the Indians."

Cynthia (to Jennifer): I completely agree with you especially about trying to work it out and also about the east becoming overpopulated.

Jennifer's initial post clearly stated her opinion and even evoked prior knowledge of American-British relations, perhaps referencing the Proclamation Line of 1763. However, all of the replies simply regurgitated her opinions without questioning the inherent problems that may have occurred without governmental regulation of westward expansion.

Another thread from the same prompt highlights a different impediment to historical discussion:

Allen: It would be a tough decision, (I don't know why I would be president anyway lol) but I would probably still let them continue to go west, however, I would tell them to try and go around the Native American Indians if possible, and absolutely no fighting or pushing them out of their homeland, or they would suffer the same consequences as if they did that to any other American. I would tell the people that they have more of a right to be here than we do, because they were here first, and even though they were different and did not live with us and were in their own tribes, they still had rights, and if we broke them, we were no different than the British trying to break our rights.

Walter (to Allen): I agree with your statements and the points you made. However I know everyone, including myself, is stating that they would make the Settlers go around or be humane to the Native Americans. It is hard to tell settlers to be humane to Native Americans but to be inhumane toward their own slaves. At that time period it seems that everyone different from the settlers, even different groups of settlers were viewed as different and inferior. People felt like they could treat people who were different than they were as inferior.

Jennifer (to Allen): I agree with that, it does sound a lot like the British trying to limit our rights.

In this instance, Allen advocates his plan for westward expansion, which relies on avoiding conflict with Native American tribes whenever possible. Then Walter raises a sophisticated point regarding the tendency of his classmates to advocate humane treatment for Native Americans while ignoring the fact that many Whites in the South owned and mistreated African American slaves during this time period.

Walter's post broaches the idea of historical understanding by shifting the conversation from a stance rooted in presentism to a critical analysis of life during the early 19th century. Unfortunately, his efforts were in vain since no one attempted to respond to his query. The lone person to contribute to this thread after Walter's post, Jennifer, chose to passively agree with Allen's comment rather than engage Walter and continue the conversation. Jennifer's actions suggest that she may have chosen to read Allen's initial post and respond without reading the entire thread up to that point.

Other evidence suggests that students did not attempt to read a majority of the posts. Referring again to Table 5.3, if the 12 questions that Mr. Harding posed are removed, his students asked 21 questions on the discussion board during the span of the course, and none of them were ever answered. The only response to a question occurred during the aforementioned exchange between Cynthia and Mr. Harding in the Reconstruction unit.

The student interviews also served to confirm this assertion. When asked how many posts they read per unit, none of the students claimed to read all of their classmates' posts. Five students admitted to reading fewer than five posts per unit; other responses ranged from "about half" to "everyone's initial post."

Lack of Teacher Participation

Prior to the start of the course, Mr. Harding told me in our interview that he felt he had to "really force the discussion board interaction. I have to force the discussion and the comments. And it almost always falls short of what I hope and anticipate to get." Yet Mr. Harding's actions before and during the course seemed to contradict this statement.

For example, he never set a required number of student posts per unit. Instead, during the initial face-to-face meeting, he simply explained the purpose of the discussion board and encouraged students to interact with each other and engage in historical discussions. However, the range of the number of posts and statements listed in Table 5.1 suggests that his students held differing interpretations of what constituted an appropriate level of participation.

In addition, when asked whether he instituted minimum word requirements on students' discussion board posts, Mr. Harding replied,

> I have not done word limits; I didn't think I would have to. I am finally realizing that I needed to do that. I model the behavior in the orientation, but what I see is that almost always some kids will meet the expectations, but most kids will immediately start falling back, giving me, you know, two to three sentence answers. You know, I am looking for deeper stuff.

A week later at the orientation session, Mr. Harding did give students a guideline of 250 words for each initial discussion board post. This requirement, however, was not listed on the syllabus or on any of the individual discussion board assignments, nor was it reinforced by Mr. Harding throughout the course. Of the 13 students in the class, only Cynthia and Brandon routinely met this standard.

Prior to the course, Mr. Harding also stated that he routinely gave feedback to students online, comparing the nature of the feedback to what students would find in the classroom:

> I am directing their learning. I am giving them feedback. I am giving them encouragement, or discouragement if they don't do a good job on it. I will answer their questions, so you see a very similar role between the classroom and the computer, you know, online environment.

Mr. Harding clarified his comments by saying that he does not feel he interacts with his online students as much as he does with his students during the regular school year. Moreover, he appeared skeptical that his online students took the time to read the feedback that he did provide them.

Although Mr. Harding may have routinely provided feedback to students when he returned homework and projects, his feedback within the discussion board occurred primarily at the start of the course with only a handful of comments occurring after the second unit. During the first unit, Mr. Harding replied to nearly every student's initial post, offering praise for a well-articulated response and questioning or asking for clarification when necessary. The following is Mr. Harding's response to Pete in that first unit:

> Good start Pete! Cities in the North and farming in the South . . . definitely a long term effect of Colonization. What about race relations? Can you see that connection? How about the issue of morality and the Puritans? Natural rights? Keep going on this one.

These comments and similar ones made to others in the class appeared to ask students to return to the topic and elaborate on their thoughts or even engage in a dialogue with Mr. Harding. However, neither Pete nor any of his classmates responded to any of Mr. Harding's posts in that first unit.

After making four posts in the second unit, Mr. Harding made only four additional posts during the rest of the course. Three of those posts were to Cynthia, who regularly provided the most detailed and lengthy posts in each unit. Only once did Mr. Harding post his thoughts regarding the question posed in a particular unit. This occurred in the Jacksonian unit and acted as a summary of the discussion to that point:

> Ok—you have made some good points. Look especially at Cynthia's summary of the problem. On one hand, you are the US President. Remember how Americans perceived Indians at this time—they were considered to be savages. You need the land. If you don't take it, someone else will. Northerners and Southerners each want to go West—for different reasons. On the other hand, the Indians were there first. They are entitled to their land. What will you do? It is a real problem . . . You can't please everyone all the time.

In addition, Mr. Harding did not seek to involve himself in his students' social conceptualization of history. As Table 5.3 shows, Mr. Harding never attempted to answer any of the 21 student questions that were posed throughout the duration of the course. This inaction contradicts his earlier statement regarding student feedback and suggests either an unwillingness to engage in his students' discussions or poor monitoring of the discussion board interaction.

Mr. Harding's decline in discussion board participation was not due to satisfaction with the quality of students' posts. On the contrary, Mr. Harding appeared despondent about the progress made by the majority of the class. In an e-mail shortly before the midterm exam, Mr. Harding wrote the following when I asked for his reaction to the discussion board participation thus far:

> It is frustrating for me. Cynthia, Walter, and Jennifer are making good use of the course. Brandon and Allen are a step down . . . but, still getting something out of the class. The others are at various levels of just easing through. My biggest frustration with myself is the lack of ability/commitment to interacting with them on the dboards.

Based on his comments, Mr. Harding appeared to share the blame for what he considered poor participation in the discussion board. Although Mr. Harding expressed regret for not actively interacting in class discussions in this e-mail, he did not increase his level of participation in the second half of the course.

LESSONS LEARNED

Although this case study paints a dismal portrait of asynchronous discussion, several lessons can be learned from the way Mr. Harding managed the course discussion boards. Here are a few tips that can increase both the frequency of students' responses to each other and the substance of their comments.

Asynchronous Communication Requires Structure and Modeling

Perhaps the greatest detriment to the quality of the course discussion in Mr. Harding's class was the fact that the students were left, for the most part, on their own to initiate, sustain, and regulate the discussions in each unit. For high school students taking their first online course, such a task is nearly impossible. What occurred were responses posted for the sake of posting, few assertions backed by evidence, and a general lack of engagement. In other words, it seems as if the students were talking *at* each other rather than *with* each other on the discussion board.

Mr. Harding's lack of attention paid to the course discussion board reinforces previous findings that suggest teacher monitoring of asynchronous communication is essential to creating a constructivist learning environment (e.g., Berge, 2002; Maor, 2003). Also affecting the quality of students' responses was Mr. Harding's failure to model appropriate discussion responses. Research has shown that students are more likely to engage in quality asynchronous discussion if they are provided a model of what a quality post should look like (e.g., DiPietro et al., 2008).

That the students producing lower quality posts and receiving poor grades on their discussion board assignments never seemed to improve the substance of their posts might indicate that they either did not understand what Mr. Harding was looking for or simply did not care. An e-mail response from Mr. Harding to a parent who questioned his son's discussion board grade lends evidence to the former, at least for some students:

> Hi again. In regard to the discussion boards on Blackboard, tell Brandon to take a look at Cynthia's comments for the last couple of units. She is consistently earning the highest marks. You should not judge Brandon by the other students. Most of the class members are not earning as high a grade as Brandon (on discussion board responses). He simply needs to add in more facts; to give more thought and insight into the answers. Even Cynthia is not giving me quite as much as I would like. However, she is setting the bar for the rest of the class.

This e-mail suggests that Brandon did not know exactly what constituted a quality post in Mr. Harding's mind. Moreover, according to Mr. Harding, none of the students seemed to be reaching his ideal vision of a satisfactory post. Yet at no point did Mr. Harding ever model what a substantive post looked like. Modeling is an effective strategy for student learning regardless of context, but it seems especially important for the success of novice online learners, who may have little experience with asynchronous academic discussions.

Along the same lines, K–12 online teachers would be wise to establish a minimum word count for student discussion board posts. More words, of course, do not necessarily equate to greater depth of understanding. Adolescents, especially those lacking intrinsic motivation, may need a word requirement to help them search for factual information from which to develop their opinions.

There exists no definitive guideline for the number of words needed to make a quality post. A guideline of a minimum of 250 words (or about one double-spaced page in Microsoft Word) for students' initial post and a minimum of 150 words for replies to classmates is usually enough to foster more substantive dialogue among students. Word requirements are an example of a relatively simple modification that teachers can make to quickly improve the quality of asynchronous discussions in their classes.

Teachers, unfortunately, also probably need to require that students reply to a certain number of their classmates' posts. Again, the exact number isn't important; rather, the point is to help stimulate dialogue by providing an incentive for the less intrinsically motivated students in the class to engage each other in conversations. Without explicit guidelines for the number of initial posts and replies, discussion boards wind up looking like what occurred in Mr. Harding's class—a lot of initial posts, but very few replies.

Create a Schedule for Posting

One of the reasons Mr. Harding's students did not engage in conversations with each other on the course discussion boards is because he did not implement a schedule for posting within each unit. His instruction was simply to reply to the prompt for that particular unit, and the expectation was that students would reply to each other and start conversations. If, however, students procrastinate and post right before the completion of a unit, then their classmates do not have much time to view and respond to their posts, which stifles opportunities for sustained discussions.

Without a set schedule, most high school students are going to procrastinate until the last minute. These students, therefore, will make posts right before the deadline and then never go back and check to see whether anyone read and responded to their posts because their attention will be on the next unit in the course. The few that post ahead of schedule will find that few of their classmates are replying to their posts, and they will eventually stop checking the discussion board as well.

An easy way to facilitate initial posts and replies is by forcing students to post on a regular schedule. Say, for example, students are expected to complete a typical unit within the span of a week. Teachers could require that students make their initial 250-word post by 5:00 p.m. on Tuesday. Then students would have until 5:00 p.m. on Wednesday to reply to classmates. Again, it is usually a good idea to establish a minimum number of replies expected of each student.

At that point, the original posters can go back to the discussion board expecting to see replies to their post, and then they can reply to the replies. Before long, a conversation has been started! By the end of the week, teachers should expect to see several substantive discussion board threads, and once students get used to this type of pattern, the discussions should develop more naturally.

Place Students into Smaller Groups

Another factor that helps determine the depth of asynchronous discussion board threads is the size of the class. Research has shown that one disadvantage of threaded discussions is that they involve a considerable amount of reading. Students often grow impatient and stop reading classmates' posts due to time constraints (e.g., Larson, 2003). In this class of only 13 students, those whom I interviewed freely admitted to not reading all of their classmates' posts in any given unit because it took up too much of their time.

Each unit, as a result, contained unequal student participation. Those who posted early received the most replies from classmates while those who posted later often had none. This unequal distribution of replies is damaging to student interaction at both ends of the spectrum. Those with no replies will obviously have difficulty engaging in a discussion (and may also feel dejected that they spent time writing a post that no one seemed to read). Those with multiple replies cannot be expected to take the time to write substantive responses to each of their classmates. In other words, student workload becomes unequal as well.

A great strategy for addressing this problem is putting students into groups of three or four students and having them post only to each other. A small number of students is more manageable, and it helps ensure that everyone's posts will be read and replied to. Students are more likely to read their classmates' posts if they are required to read only three additional posts as opposed to ten or more. Teachers could then rotate groups throughout the span of a course to ensure that students are being exposed to a variety of perspectives.

Putting students in smaller groups usually *increases* total participation when compared to asking students to participate in whole-class discussions. The reasons for this are similar to why some students do not like to participate in whole-class face-to-face discussions. Many students feel intimidated by posting in a forum where so many people will read their post. A small group makes these shier students feel safer, and as a result, they tend to post more frequently.

Provide Students with Ammunition for Their Discussions

Although the majority of unit discussion threads in Mr. Harding's class operated in the manner I described above, there was one exception to this rule. In the slavery unit, Mr. Harding provided his students with several primary sources and then divided the class into two groups: Southern plantation owners and Northern abolitionists. He then had students engage in a mock debate over the merits of slavery based on their antebellum roles.

As Table 5.4 shows, the slavery discussion board garnered considerably more total posts, replies, and substantive statements than any other unit.

Table 5.4. Number of Substantive and Nonsubstantive Statements by Unit

	Nonsubstantive (-)	Substantive (+)	Difference
Colonization	109	47	-62
Revolution	88	43	-45
Articles of Confederation	35	44	+9
Jacksonian	46	38	-8
Slavery	99	194	+95
Reconstruction	77	44	-33
Industrialization	114	63	-51
Imperialism/WWI	74	84	+10
Great Depression	164	33	-131
WWII	86	87	+1
Civil Rights	102	23	-79

The following thread from the slavery unit provides an example of the depth that was created simply by giving students primary sources on which they could base their arguments:

> *Walter*: As a Southern planter I support slavery. The main points for my position are: 1) I am providing a safer and more secure environment for the African slave, 2) My slaves join my community on the plantation not so much as workers but as part of a larger family. I do not treat my slaves

as property, 3) I treat my slaves humanely. I give them rewards, 4) Because the Bible does not condemn slavery it is alright to own slaves, 5) The slave is are freer than most Americans.[4]

Allen (to Walter): I'll show you how your wrong in each point of supporting slavery:

1. You have no idea whether their way of life before being brought over here forcibly/by trickery was better or not. I don't think hard work and poor living conditions, death and torture are much better than cannibalism, and most slave owners did not feed them adequately enough, especially compared to their harsh workload. Besides, when the colonists first started bringing them over here, it was not their intent to make their life any better.
2. Just because you say they are equal, doesn't make it true. They can never even hope to be equal even if they are free. Just the fact that they are slaves deny them the three basic rights: life (many children died due to disease in poor living conditions), liberty (they were not free, they had to spend the whole day in the plantations, without breaks, and with no rights to say anything to their masters), pursuit of happiness (I would definitely not be happy as a slave)
3. Most slave owners treated them very poorly. They had very filthy living conditions and had disease and malnutrition that killed many children and were not treated with respect. They whipped them, even pregnant women, and even if you claim to be nicer than the next slave owner, that is not a very good excuse.
4. The Bible is the perfect literature <u>against</u> slavery; God made all humans equal, and should be treated equally. The Pharoah, who had thousands of slaves whipped them and ruled them and they had to work in the hot sun all day long, just for the Pharoah own wealth and power (sort of like the slaves in the 1850s). And the Pharoah was brought to justice by Moses (the abolitionists) and God.
5. They were just the opposite, they weren't comfortable at all, and were not free to do a thing. I don't think any kind of slave with no hope for any kind of future would have any kind of 'peace of mind' especially while working or being whipped.

Amy (to Allen): Slaves definitely didn't have a great life in the south, but it was better than living in the north. They just lived on streets and had no where to work, no where to live, or eat. They couldn't even go to church without being degraded. In the south they were guaranteed a life they could make due with and they were able to make peace with many people.

Allen (to Amy): I'm not against the North, just slavery. It was because of slavery that slaves were looked down upon in the North and didn't have anywhere to eat, sleep, etc. Even though the people were fighting slavery, they didn't like slaves or just though they were inferior because of slavery.

Hunter (to Allen's 1st post): In the Bible it does say that but people in the north own stores and they have people working for them and some of the owners do not treat their workers good. I mean you guys just don't call it slavery.

Cynthia (to Allen's 1st post): There were many slave owners who made sure that the work loads that were given were fair and that people such as women, children, and the aged had less loads if any at all. Not all slaveowners treated their slaves poorly, for one their were often rewards for good work and behavior plus many treated them like family so they were very well take care of. Many slaves actually loved their owners very much too. And while I know in the bible it talks about equalness, there is also a lot of servants in the bible so you can't say the bible strictly says that slavery or servanthood is wrong.

Pete (to Allen's 1st post): yes they may just be basic slaves, but just because they are slaves doesn't mean they can't have rights. They don't have rights because they are slaves, and they are slaves because southern plantes only care for themselves. They would even be here if you hadn't taken them from their home land and broke up their families

Jennifer (to Walter): I find the different accounts of slavery interesting. One side, the south, says that slaves were treated right and that they lived a better life. Conversely, based on what the abolitionists saw, slaves were treated like dirt and lived terrible lives. Personally, I would be much happier free, rather than enslaved, even if that meant less food and certainty of shelter. That is probably how many slaves and former slaves felt.

Pete (to Walter): Slavery is morally wrong and physically wrong. People die every day because of excusiating pain they are put through. Our founding fathers left England because the king treated them like slaves, but yet we are doing the same thing to these people.

While the placing of students into roles, particularly that of a plantation owner, may be unsettling to some, situating the discussion into a debate format using primary sources appeared to spark student creativity. In contrast to the Jacksonian threads shown earlier, this discussion had several levels, and multiple conversations were being held simultaneously. More importantly, the primary sources allowed these students to partially reconstruct the slavery argument as it existed in the 19th century, a fact that Jennifer noted in her summary of the dialogue up to that point.

When asked how they liked the slavery discussion, nearly all of the students claimed to enjoy the debate. Alex specifically mentioned the use of primary sources, citing that the resources made it "easier to debate and bring up a lot of arguments." Cynthia agreed and stated that she enjoyed the debate because it "kind of got people to write more." The only negative comments about the debate came from three students who were assigned as plantation owners and complained that they were forced to defend a position they did not advocate.

If teachers do not provide students with concrete data to use when formulating arguments, then they should not be surprised when students' posts consist almost entirely of broad generalities and unsubstantiated opinions. Also, putting students into specific roles allows for an element of creativity and forces students to focus their arguments. When students are given incentive to read others' posts and consider alternative points of view, there is a better chance that more substantive conversations will develop.

Teachers Must Be Active Participants

Perhaps the most obvious lesson gleaned from Mr. Harding's class is the importance of the teacher in facilitating substantive asynchronous discussions. From providing appropriate structure to modeling what constitutes a quality post, teachers are essential to the success of student interaction online. However, their role as facilitator does not end in the planning stages. Teachers also need to be active participants within class discussions.

As with classroom discussions, the goal is for students to do most of the "talking." This is especially true in online courses, where the vast majority of information students receive will be from text-based sources read on their own. Teachers should be cognizant of the possibility of monopolizing asynchronous discussions. When teachers post on a discussion board, there is a natural tendency among students to assume that the teacher is the expert in the "room" and gravitate toward his or her post, often at the expense of their classmates' posts.

Teachers, therefore, should refrain from posting too much. Yet that does not mean that the discussion board should be out of sight or out of mind. As in the classroom, teachers need to be active monitors of student discussions. They should be ready to answer students' questions, offer alternative viewpoints, and clarify incorrect statements. None of this seemed to occur in Mr. Harding's course, especially after the first couple of units.

Based on my analysis of his discussion boards, Mr. Harding failed to be an active participant within his students' discussions. The 21 unanswered student questions are evidence enough that the discussion board was not being monitored with any sort of regularity. Especially when working with adolescents, who may not be intrinsically motivated to discuss academic issues with their peers, active monitoring of student discussions is the only way to ensure quality interactions. Once students realize that no one is holding them accountable for their posts, they have little incentive to develop thoughtful responses.

SUMMARY

This chapter provided a case study of a K–12 online course in which students were required to regularly participate in asynchronous discussions but were given few guidelines by their teacher. The resulting discussions that occurred in this course were rarely substantive and often carried by only a handful of students. In order to make asynchronous communication meaningful, teachers can use the following strategies:

- Create a regular schedule for posting.
- Model what a quality post looks like.
- Implement minimum word requirements for posts and replies.
- Implement a minimum number of replies each student should make.
- Place students into smaller groups.
- Provide students with ammunition for their posts.

Implementing these strategies can quickly improve both the number and quality of posts in most K–12 online courses.

NOTES

This chapter was adapted from my 2008 article "Facilitating Historical Discussions Using Asynchronous Communication: The Role of the Teacher," in *Theory and Research in Social Education, 36*, pp. 317–355.

1. The Cold War unit did not have a discussion board assignment.
2. None of the posts from students or Mr. Harding has been changed to improve grammar or spelling.
3. Two students, Beth and Rebecca, maintained technical problems through the course and, therefore, had limited access to the discussion board and rarely interacted with the other students in the course. Their discussion assignments were submitted directly to Mr. Harding via e-mail or the Blackboard digital dropbox.
4. For the sake of brevity, I am including only the main points of Walter's post. Walter extensively backed each point with verbatim quotations from the primary source material.

Chapter Six

Where Do We Go From Here?

For online learning to serve as a sustainable alternative to K–12 classroom instruction, teachers need to continually learn more about online pedagogy. K–12 online education remains in its infancy, and there is still much we do not know about how to create effective online learning environments for adolescents. This chapter highlights some of the issues that will become increasingly important as more districts begin moving curricula online.

THE IMPORTANCE OF ONLINE PROFESSIONAL DEVELOPMENT

As K–12 online learning becomes more ubiquitous in the United States, there will be a greater need for preservice and practicing teachers to specialize in online pedagogy. It makes little sense for teachers to be placed in environments in which they have little experience and then expect them to teach like a seasoned veteran. For teachers facing the prospect of online instruction, it would be wise to seek professional development before attempting to create or teach an online course.

The issue, however, is that colleges and universities have not kept up with the times. Only now are teacher training programs starting to incorporate courses and programs specifically designed to train K–12 teachers for online learning. Here is a brief look at the current state of online teacher preparation in the United States.

The Rise of Online Learning Degree Programs

The next logical step in the evolution of K–12 online learning is for states to develop licensure options specifically designed for online instruction. Currently, four states (Wisconsin, Michigan, Georgia, and Idaho) offer either endorsements in online instruction or require online teachers to take a minimum amount of professional development in online pedagogy in order to teach online. In addition, a handful of universities throughout the United States offer either graduate or continuing education certificates in online teaching (Barbour, Siko, Gross, & Waddell, 2013).

By requiring licensure specific to online instruction for those wishing to teach online, states would be taking a major step toward ensuring quality K–12 online courses. Currently, however, few online instructors have had any formal training in online pedagogy. In a study of K–12 online teachers across the United States, Archambault and Crippen (2009) found that of the 596 teachers surveyed, less than 1% reported holding a degree in distance education.

Right now, all that is required in order to teach online is to be a content expert. As Mr. Harding's experience shows, that is often not enough to ensure a successful online experience for students. Requiring teachers hold a license for online instruction not only will help improve the quality of online courses, it will also help legitimize online learning as a reputable form of instruction within K–12 education.

The one problem with online licensure is that just as it is not enough to simply be a content expert to be a successful online teacher, it is also not enough to simply be versed in online learning theory. Online teachers also need to have deep knowledge of the subject(s) they teach. Even if a course is designed by a content expert, student learning will suffer if the person managing the course is not well versed in content. In other words, states and districts need to establish guidelines on the requirements for teaching online that include both content and pedagogical training.

States can also help improve the quality of K–12 online education by providing incentives for preservice teachers to become versed in both a content area and online learning theory. Many states and universities have begun to offer online pedagogy as an add-on licensure option for students who are already receiving secondary licensure in a content area. Although this option may require some time and money, having the additional licensure in online pedagogy would make teachers more marketable to future employers and well prepared to teach online.

Unfortunately, several of the leading authorities on teacher accreditation and licensure, such as the National Council for Accreditation of Teacher Education (NCATE) or the Teacher Education Accreditation Council (TEAC), have yet to develop standards specifically for the preparation of K–12 online teachers (Kennedy & Archambault, 2012). Other professional organizations, however, have adopted such standards. These organizations include the following (Kennedy, 2010):

- The International Society for Technology in Education (ISTE, 2008)

- The Southern Regional Education Board (SREB, 2006)
- National Education Association (NEA, 2006)
- International Association for K–12 Online Learning (iNACOL, 2008)

All of these organizations address both the dispositions and skills required of online teachers and would be useful as a starting point for states to develop online licensure standards. These organizations would also be of interest to teachers as they seek ongoing professional development opportunities.

The State of Online Teacher Training in the United States

Training in online instructional theory is essential to successfully teaching online. The case study of Mr. Harding's class is a perfect example of the poor educational experience that can occur when exceptional classroom teachers are asked to teach online without any formal training. Unfortunately, districts are limited in their ability to train prospective online teachers.

According to the National Education Association (2006), "all new educators should be equipped to instruct online" (p. 22). Yet within the United States, only a handful of universities offer programs specifically designed for training preservice teachers for online pedagogy. The scope and quality of these programs vary from institution to institution, but most offer both courses on online learning theory and field experiences where preservice teachers can partner with experienced online instructors (Barbour et al., 2013; Kennedy & Archambault, 2012).

One of the first such programs began at Iowa State University and was modeled after nationally recognized traditional teacher education programs. In this program, students receive 45 hours of training in virtual pedagogy, spend 12 hours on course design, and participate in up to 24 hours of field experiences (Barbour et al., 2013; Davis & Roblyer, 2005). Kennedy and Archambault (2012) also report that similar programs have been developed in universities in Florida (in conjunction with the FVHS), North Dakota, and South Dakota.

Kennedy and Archambault (2012) found ten additional universities where online training of preservice teachers was in the planning stages. The extent to which online pedagogy was to be addressed varied at these institutions, however. In some cases, the training consisted of one assignment within the context of an educational technology course whereas in other institutions, students were given the option to complete their student teaching in an online environment.

Although it is encouraging that more teacher education programs have begun to incorporate online instruction into their curricula, this transition is moving too slowly to keep up with the demand for K–12 online education in the United States. The variation in what universities consider to be "good" online teacher preparation also suggests that the field knows relatively little about how to best train teachers for virtual pedagogy. The good news for practitioners is that colleges and universities have recognized the need for increased training for online pedagogy, and these types of programs should increase in both number and quality in the upcoming decades.

It is clear that what teachers need to learn and be able to do in order to be successful professionals in the 21st century must include training in online teaching and learning. Moreover, this cannot be done within the context of one assignment or even one course. At a minimum, one must spend considerable time learning about online pedagogical theories as well as experiencing online instruction firsthand.

Practicum and student-teaching experiences have become a required element of most teacher education programs, and it stands to reason that preservice and practicing teachers would need these types of experiences before being asked to teach online (Kennedy & Archambault, 2012). Although the options for these types of professional development opportunities for practicing teachers are currently limited, teachers should seek them out if possible. Having training in how to effectively teach online will not only make one's online instruction stronger, it will make the entire experience more satisfying for everyone involved.

CREATING ONLINE LEARNING FOR ALL

As a field, we know very little about the viability of K–12 online learning to meet the needs of learners with special needs. For online programs to be successful, however, it is imperative that teachers take steps to address ways to ensure virtual classrooms can be considered "least restrictive environments" for student learning. The following questions should be considered by teachers before moving courses online, or at least before eliminating any face-to-face options for students:

- How can teachers adapt their online instruction to meet the needs of students with reading disabilities?
- How will teachers and parents know whether individualized education plan (IEP) provisions are being carried out online?
- If IEPs were originally written for face-to-face classrooms, will they need to be rewritten for online courses?
- How will students be able to receive help from special education teachers if needed?
- How will courses be adapted for students with physical disabilities (e.g., deafness, blindness, etc.)?

Many of these same concerns also apply to ELL students. Many of the texts used in online courses will be written in English, and students will be expected to read them without the help of an ELL teacher. Many parents of ELL students are also not native English speakers and may not be able to offer assistance if students struggle with assignments at home.

The North American Council for Online Learning (NACOL) argues that online instruction can be adapted for nearly all learners as long as courses are planned with the needs of exceptional learners in mind (Rose & Blomeyer, 2007). Some adaptations are simple; for example, any videos used in an online course should have accompanying transcripts for learners with auditory impairments. For more complex needs, technology offers a wealth of possibilities. For example, screen readers—web browsers that speak text—could be used to aid learners with visual impairments, and a nontraditional mouse could be used for students with motor control issues.

Not only is adapting courses for exceptional learners the morally acceptable course of action, it is also the law. Teachers need to ensure that all of their online courses are accessible, especially if they choose to offer online-only options for certain courses. The mandates that govern public education in the United States (e.g., Equal Educational Opportunity Act, Individuals with Disabilities Education Act, and the *Lau v Nichols* decision) remain just as relevant online as they do in face-to-face classrooms.[1]

Adapting courses for exceptional learners should be the first step toward greater access, but it should not be the only one. Teachers should continually assess the quality of their online instruction to ensure that all learners are reaping the same educational benefits. NACOL (Rose & Blomeyer, 2007) argues that the type of data that teachers collect from their online courses will help them make appropriate decisions regarding making online instruction more affirming of diversity. They specifically list the following questions for teachers to consider when assessing the quality of their courses:

- Can the data that is collected be disaggregated by race and ethnicity?
- Can the data that is collected be disaggregated by poverty and/or socioeconomic status?
- Can the data that is collected be disaggregated by disability (e.g., students diagnosed as having a documented exceptionality)?
- Can the data that is collected be disaggregated by language proficiency?
- How does the proportion of students from these subgroups compare to the proportion of students from these subgroups within the entire school and/or district enrollment?

Positive change first starts with accurate information. Therefore, it is essential that teachers develop procedures for collecting student data and then using that data to improve their programs, in terms of both quality and access.

Certainly, test scores and other objective measures are important indicators of student and teacher success. Issues of access and cultural diversity, however, also need to be assessed. Often, qualitative measures are the best way to learn what deficiencies may exist within a course. Students tend to be brutally honest, so giving students regular opportunities to safely share their thoughts about the structure of a course may be one way to ensure that teachers are meeting the needs of all of their learners.

What makes adapting online learning for exceptional learners and learners from diverse cultural backgrounds a virtual black box is the dearth of knowledge about the success of these students in K–12 online courses. Although some insight can be gleaned from research conducted with these populations in online higher education courses, it would be a mistake to assume that the two contexts transfer seamlessly.

For example, there exists a fairly extensive research base about the experiences of minority students, especially African Americans, in online higher education, but one cannot generalize too much about K–12 online learning from this line of research. Comparing the experiences of students from minority groups who attend college with those of minority groups in K–12 environments could prove to be quite different. Regardless, attention to access and equity in online education should be an essential aspect of teachers' assessments of their online courses.

ADDRESSING TECHNOLOGICAL INEQUITIES

Although less attention is being paid to the digital divide in this era of iPhones and wireless Internet, there are still communities in the United States where computer and Internet use remains a luxury. Statistics that show most households, even those in low socioeconomic areas, have computer and Internet access can be misleading. These statistics rarely acknowledge that students may be working with a dial-up connection or having to share one computer with the rest of an entire household.

According to NACOL, "Public schools that operate educational programs available only through students' own computers are not truly accessible" (Rose & Blomeyer, 2007, p. 3). The fate of K–12 online learning, therefore, rests hand in hand with the ability of teachers and school districts to provide opportunities for students with limited Internet access to get online and work under the same conditions as their classmates. Even if districts provide laptops to students taking online courses, that does not necessarily solve problems related to access. Without a high-speed Internet connection, for example, students will be at a disadvantage in all aspects of online learning.

Obviously, one potential solution to this problem would be to make libraries and computer labs in students' home schools available for regular use. Schools, however, cannot remain open all of the time. Another option that teachers may wish to pursue is seeking help from the community (public libraries, local universities, etc.). Prior research has shown that the development of community technology centers has the potential to diminish the effects of the digital divide in low-income, urban communities (e.g, Servon & Nelson, 2001). If community agencies could designate times at night and during weekends for students to work on their online coursework, it could alleviate many of the access problems they may face at home.

FINAL THOUGHTS

Online learning has been considered by many to be the next frontier of K–12 public education in the United States. At some point, however, we have to stop looking at online learning as the instruction of the future and admit that the era of K–12 online learning is already upon us. Millions of adolescents are taking online courses as part of their middle and high school curricula, and that number is only going to rise in the coming years.

The issues raised in this chapter are only a fraction of the additional considerations that teachers must take into account as public education moves online. Many of the challenges have not yet been discovered, and even as we solve those, new ones will continue to arise in the wake of new technologies or governmental mandates. Yet that is the nature of public education in the United States; changes occur, and educators and students adapt.

For many readers, the possibilities discussed in this book may be frightening. It is natural to be apprehensive of the unknown. Yet being a part of the next wave in public education is also exciting. Regardless of how one feels personally about online education, it is most certainly on the horizon, and the sooner educators embrace the reality of the situation, the better off they will be. Instead of rallying against online education, the focus of teachers and administrators should be on responding to the challenges associated with making online learning a viable learning option for all students.

As I have attempted to illustrate throughout this book, there is considerable potential in online learning for K–12 education. This potential will be recognized, however, only if teachers put the instructional needs of their students ahead of any desire to cut costs. If online learning saves money in the long run, that is a bonus. The impetus for teachers wishing to move curricula online, however, should be to provide a medium that allows more students to obtain a quality education than ever before. If that remains the focus, then online learning may very well equal or supersede the learning that is occurring in our best face-to-face classes.

I certainly hope that this book has been helpful to those wishing to start online learning programs within their districts or seeking to improve ones that currently exist. That said, I am sure that once teachers become immersed in online education, issues will arise that I did not cover in these pages. When that happens, do not hesitate to contact me (awjourne@uncg.edu). I may not always have the answer, but I promise to respond and will help the best that I can.

NOTE

1. The North American Council for Online Learning (Rose & Blomeyer, 2007) provides an extensive list of mandates that need to be considered when determining whether online courses are legally compliant. They include the following:

Equal Educational Opportunity Act of 1974: http://uscode.house.gov/download/pls/20C39.txt

Title IX of the Educational Amendments of 1972: http://www.dol.gov/oasam/regs/statutes/titleix.htm#.UJFxA66vPXM

Title VI of the Civil Rights Act of 1964: http://www2.ed.gov/policy/rights/reg/ocr/edlite-34cfr100.html

Lau v Nichols Decision: http://www.law.cornell.edu/supct/html/historics/USSC_CR_0414_0563_ZS.html

Individuals with Disabilities Education Act: http://idea.ed.gov/

Section 504 of the Rehabilitation Act of 1973: http://www.dol.gov/oasam/regs/statutes/sec504.htm#.UJFyIa6vPXM

References

Alabama State Board of Education. (2008). *Alabama administrative code rule 290-3-1-.02(12) for online courses*. Retrieved from http://www.adph.org/tpts/assets/schoolpolicy.pdf

Allen, I. E., & Seaman, J. (2011). *Going the distance: Online education in the United States, 2011.* Sloan Consortium. Retrieved from http://www.onlinelearningsurvey.com/reports/goingthedistance.pdf

Archambault, L., & Crippen, K. (2009). K–12 distance educators at work: Who's teaching online across the United States. *Journal of Research on Technology in Education, 41*, 363–391.

Barbour, M. K. (2007). *What are they doing and how are they doing it? Rural student experiences in virtual schooling.* (Unpublished doctoral dissertation). University of Georgia, Athens, GA.

Barbour, M. K. (2008). Secondary students' perceptions of web-based learning. *Quarterly Review of Distance Education, 9*, 357–371.

Barbour, M. K. (2009). Today's student and virtual schooling: The reality, the challenges, the promise ... *Journal of Distance Learning, 13*, 5–25.

Barbour, M. K. (2010). Researching K–12 online learning: What do we know and what should we examine? *Distance Learning, 7*(2), 6–12.

Barbour, M. K., & Reeves, T. C. (2009). The reality of virtual schools: A review of the literature. *Computers and Education, 52*, 402–416.

Barbour, M. K., Siko, J., Gross, E., & Waddell, K. (2013). Virtually unprepared: Examining the preparation of K–12 online teachers. In R. Hartshorne, T. L. Heafner, & T. M. Petty (Eds.), *Teacher education programs and online learning tools: Innovations in teacher preparation* (pp. 60–81). Hershey, PA: IGI Global.

Bassoppo-Moyo, T. C. (2006). Evaluating elearning: A front-end, process and post hoc approach. *International Journal of Instructional Media, 33*, 7–22.

Bates, T. (2000). *Managing technological change: Strategies for college and university leaders.* San Francisco, CA: Jossey-Bass.

Battalio, J. (2009). Success in distance education: Do learning styles and multiple formats matter? *American Journal of Distance Education, 23*, 71–87.

Bender, S. A. (2010). Attendance policy and truancy procedures of an online school. *Distance Learning, 7*(2), 51–55.

Berge, Z. L. (2002). Active, interactive, and reflective elearning. *Quarterly Review of Distance Education, 3*, 181–190.

Bernard, R. M., Abrami, P. C., Lou, Y., Borokhovski, E., Wade, A., Wozney, L., & Huang, B. (2004). How does distance education compare to classroom education? A meta-analysis of the empirical literature. *Review of Educational Research, 74*, 379–439.

Bernard, R. M., Brauer, A., Abrami, P. C., & Surkes, M. (2004). The development of a questionnaire for predicting online learning achievement. *Distance Education, 25*, 31–47.

Blaylock, T. H., & Newman, J. W. (2005). The impact of computer-based secondary education. *Education, 125*, 373–384.

Blignaut, A. S., & Trollip, S. R. (2003). Measuring faculty participation in asynchronous discussion forums. *Journal of Education for Business, 78*, 347–353.

Boling, E. C., Hough, M., Krinsky, H., Saleem, H., & Stevens, M. (2012). Cutting the distance in distance education: Perspectives on what promotes positive, online learning experiences. *Internet and Higher Education, 15*, 118–126.

Bradley, C. L., & Renzulli, L. A. (2011). The complexity of non-completion: Being pushed or pulled to drop out of high school. *Social Forces, 90*, 521–545.

Bruce, B. C. (2004). Maintaining the affordances of traditional education long distance. In C. Haythornthwaite & M. M. Kazmer (Eds.), *Learning, culture and community in online education: Research and practice* (pp. 19–32). New York, NY: Peter Lang.

Cavanaugh, C. S., Barbour, M. K., & Clark, T. (2009). Research and practice in K–12 online learning: A review of open access literature. *International Review of Research in Open and Distance Learning, 10*, 1–22.

Chakraborty, J., & Bosman, M. M. (2005). Measuring the digital divide in the United States: Race, income, and personal computer ownership. *Professional Geographer, 57*, 395–410.

Chen, D. W., & McGeehan, P. (2012, May 1). Social media rules limit New York student-teacher contact. *The New York Times*. Retrieved from http://www.nytimes.com/2012/05/02/nyregion/social-media-rules-for-nyc-school-staff-limits-contact-with-students.html?_r=1&pagewanted=all

Clark, R. C., & Mayer, R. E. (2008). *E-learning and the science of instruction: Proven guidelines for consumers and designers of multimedia learning* (2nd ed.). San Francisco, CA: Pfeiffer.

Conceição, S. C. O. (2006). Faculty lived experiences in the online environment. *Adult Education Quarterly, 57*, 1–20.

Conceição, S. C. O., & Drummond, S. B. (2005). Online learning in secondary education: A new frontier. *Educational Considerations, 33*, 31–37.

Conceição, S. C. O., & Lehman, R. M. (2011). *Managing instructor workload: Strategies for balance and success*. San Francisco, CA: Jossey-Bass.

Coombs, N. (2005). Transcending distances and differences with online learning. In G. Kearsley (Ed.), *Online learning: Personal reflections on the transformation of education* (pp. 53–65). Englewood Cliffs, NJ: Educational Technology Publications.

Coryell, J. E., & Chlup, D. T. (2007). Implementing e-learning components with adult English language learners: Vital factors and lessons learned. *Computer Assisted Language Learning, 20*, 263–278.

Davidson-Shivers, G. V., Morris, S. B., & Sriwongkol, T. (2003). Gender differences: Are they diminished in online discussions? *International Journal on E-Learning, 2*, 29–36.

Davies, J., & Graff, M. (2005). Performance in e-learning: Online participation and student grades. *British Journal of Educational Technology, 36*, 657–663.

Davis, N. E., & Roblyer, M. D. (2005). Preparing teachers for the "schools that technology built": Evaluation of a program to train teachers for virtual schooling. *Journal of Research on Technology in Education, 37*, 399–409.

Debuse, J. C. W., Hede, A., & Lawley, M. (2009). Learning efficacy of simultaneous audio and onscreen text in online lectures. *Australasian Journal of Educational Technology, 25*, 748–762.

DeTure, M. (2004). Cognitive style and self-efficacy: Predicting student success in online distance education. *American Journal of Distance Education, 18*, 21–38.

Dewstow, R., & Wright, N. (2005). Secondary school students, online learning, and external support in New Zealand. *Computers in the Schools, 22*, 111–122.

DiBiase, D. (2000). Is distance teaching more work or less work? *American Journal of Distance Education, 14*, 6–20.

DiBiase, D. (2004). The impact of increasing enrollment on faculty workload and student satisfaction over time. *Journal of Asynchronous Learning Networks, 8*, 45–60.

DiPietro, M., Ferdig, R. E., Black, E. W., & Preston, M. (2008). Best practices in teaching K–12 online: Lessons learned from Michigan Virtual School teachers. *Journal of Interactive Online Learning, 7*, 10–35.

Dodge, B. (1995). Webquests: A technique for Internet-based learning. *Distance Educator, 1*(2), 10–13.

Dressman, M., Journell, W., Babcock, A., Weatherup, N., & Makhoukh, A. (in press). Toward technology-mediated transcultural education: Learning from a discussion of politics and culture between American and Moroccan students. *International Journal of Social Education*.

Enger, K. B. (2006). Minorities and online higher education. *Educause Quarterly, 29*(4), 7–8.

Fine, M. (1991). *Framing dropouts: Notes on the politics of an urban public high school*. Albany, NY: State University of New York Press.

Florida Virtual School. (2012). Quick facts. Retrieved from http://www.flvs.net/areas/aboutus/Pages/QuickFactsaboutFLVS.aspx

Fox, E., & Riconscente, M. (2008). Metacognition and self-regulation in James, Piaget, and Vygotsky. *Educational Psychology Review, 20*, 373–389.

Friend, B., & Johnston, S. (2005). Florida Virtual School: A choice for all students. In Z. L. Berge & T. Clark (Eds.), *Virtual schools: Planning for success* (pp. 97–117). New York, NY: Teachers College Press.

Gable, R. A., Bullock, L. M., & Evans, W. H. (2006). Changing perspectives on alternative schooling for children and adolescents with challenging behavior. *Preventing School Failure, 51*, 5–9.

Garrison, D. R., & Anderson, T. (2003). *E-learning in the 21st century: A framework for research and practice*. London, UK: RoutledgeFalmer.

Giroux, H., & Purpel, D. (Eds.). (1983). *The hidden curriculum and moral education: Deception or discovery?* Berkeley, CA: McCutchan Publishing.

Githens, R. P., Crawford, F. L., & Sauer, T. M. (2010). *Online occupational education in community colleges: Prevalence and contextual factors*. National Research Center for Career and Technical Education, University of Louisville, Louisville, KY. Retrieved from http://136.165.122.102/UserFiles/File/Tech_Reports/Githens_Online_Occupational_Education.pdf

Greenhow, C., Walker, J. D., & Kim, S. (2010). Millennial learners and net-savvy teens? Examining Internet use among low-income students. *Journal of Computing in Teacher Education, 26*, 63–68.

Haythornthwaite, C. (2007). Digital divide and e-learning. In R. Andrews & C. Haythornthwaite (Eds.), *The Sage handbook of e-learning research* (pp. 97–118). London, UK: Sage.

Haythornthwaite, C., & Bregman, A. (2004). Affordances of persistent conversation: Promoting communities that work. In C. Haythornthwaite, & M. M. Kazmer (Eds.), *Learning, culture and community in online education: Research and practice* (pp. 129–143). New York, NY: Peter Lang.

Haythornthwaite, C., & Kazmer, M. M. (Eds.). (2004). *Learning, culture and community in online education: Research and practice*. New York, NY: Peter Lang.

Haythornthwaite, C., Kazmer, M. M., Robins, J., & Shoemaker, S. (2004). Community development among distance learners: Temporal and technological dimensions. In C. Haythornthwaite, & M. M. Kazmer (Eds.), *Learning, culture and community in online education: Research and practice* (pp. 35–57). New York, NY: Peter Lang.

Herring, L. C., & Clevenger-Schmertzing, L. (2007). Online high school world history: Does interaction make a difference? *Social Studies Research and Practice, 2*, 419–437.

Horton, W. (2006). *E-learning by design*. San Francisco, CA: Pfeiffer.

Hoskins, S. L., & van Hooff, J. C. (2005). Motivation and ability: Which students use online learning and what influence does it have on their achievement? *British Journal of Educational Technology, 36*, 177–192.

Hou, H., & Wu, S. (2011). Analyzing the social knowledge construction behavioral patterns of an online synchronous collaborative discussion instructional activity using an instant messaging tool: A case study. *Computers and Education, 57*, 1459–1468.

Howe, N., & Strauss, W. (2007). *Millennials go to college* (2nd ed.). Great Falls, VA: Life-Course Associates.

Hrastinski, S. (2008). Asynchronous and synchronous e-learning. *Educause Quarterly, 31*(4), 51–55.

Idaho State Board of Education. (2011). *IDAPA 08, Title 02, Chapter 02.* Retrieved from http://www.legislature.idaho.gov/legislation/2011/S1184.pdf

Im, Y., & Lee, O. (2004). Pedagogical implications of online discussion for preservice teacher training. *Journal of Research on Technology in Education, 36*, 155–170.

International Association for K–12 Online Learning. (2008). *National Standards for quality online teaching.* Retrieved from http://www.inacol.org/cms/wp-content/uploads/2013/02/iNACOL_TeachingStandardsv2.pdf

International Society for Technology in Education. (2008). *National educational technology standards (NETS*T) and performance indicators for teachers.* Retrieved from http://www.iste.org/Content/NavigationMenu/NETS/ForTeachers/2008Standards/NETS_for_Teachers_2008.htm

Journell, W. (2007). The inequities of the digital divide: Is e-learning a solution? *E-Learning, 4*, 138–149.

Journell, W. (2008). Facilitating historical discussions using asynchronous communication: The role of the teacher. *Theory and Research in Social Education, 36*, 317–355.

Journell, W. (2010). Perceptions of e-learning in secondary education: A viable alternative to classroom instruction or a way to bypass engaged learning? *Educational Media International, 47*, 69–81.

Journell, W. (2012a). Ideological homogeneity, school leadership, and political intolerance in secondary education: A study of three high schools during the 2008 presidential election. *Journal of School Leadership, 22*, 569–599.

Journell, W. (2012b). Walk, don't run—to online learning. *Phi Delta Kappan, 93*(7), 46–50.

Journell, W., Beeson, M. W., Crave, J. J., Gomez, M., Linton, J. N., & Taylor, M. O. (2013). Training teachers for virtual classrooms: A description of an experimental course in online pedagogy. In R. Hartshorne, T. L. Heafner, & T. M. Petty (Eds.), *Teacher education programs and online learning tools: Innovations in teacher preparation* (pp. 120–143). Hershey, PA: IGI Global.

Jun, J. (2005). Understanding e-dropout. *International Journal on E-Learning, 4*, 229–240.

Kalyanpur, M., & Kirmani, M. H. (2005). Diversity and technology: Classroom implications of the digital divide. *Journal of Special Education Technology, 20*(4), 9–18.

Kanuka, H., & Anderson, T. (1998). Online social exchange, discord, and knowledge construction. *Journal of Distance Education, 13*, 57–74.

Kapitzke, C., & Pendergast, D. (2005). Virtual schooling service: Productive pedagogies or pedagogical possibilities? *Teachers College Record, 107*, 1626–1651.

Keeler, C. G., & Horney, M. (2007). Online course designs: Are special needs being met? *American Journal of Distance Education, 21*, 61–75.

Kelly, S. (2007). The contours of tracking in North Carolina. *The High School Journal, 90*, 15–31.

Kennedy, K. (2010). Cross-reference of online teaching standards and the development of quality teachers for 21st century learning environments. *Distance Learning, 7*(2), 21–28.

Kennedy, K., & Archambault, L. (2012). Offering preservice teachers field experiences in K–12 online learning: A national survey of teacher education programs. *Journal of Teacher Education, 63*, 185–200.

Kickul, G., & Kickul, J. (2006). Closing the gap: Impact of student productivity and learning goal orientation on e-learning outcomes. *International Journal on E-Learning, 5*, 361–372.

Lange, C. M., & Sletten, S. J. (2002). *Alternative education: A brief history and research synthesis.* Alexandria, VA: National Association of State Directors of Special Education.

Larreamendy-Joerns, J., & Leinhardt, G. (2006). Going the distance with online education. *Review of Educational Research, 76*, 567–605.

Larson, B. E. (2003). Comparing face-to-face discussion and electronic discussion: A case study from high school social studies. *Theory and Research in Social Education, 31*, 347–365.

Levin, B. B., He, Y., & Robbins, H. H. (2006). Comparative analysis of preservice teachers' reflective thinking in synchronous versus asynchronous online case discussions. *Journal of Technology and Teacher Education, 14*, 439–460.

Lewis, C. W., Dugan, J. J., Winokur, M. A., & Cobb, R. B. (2005). The effects of block scheduling on high school academic achievement. *NASSP Bulletin, 89*, 72–87.

Lim, C. (2001). Computer self-efficacy, academic self-concept, and other predictors of satisfaction and future participation of adult distance learners. *American Journal of Distance Education, 15*, 41–52.

Liu, F., Black, E., Algina, J., Cavanaugh, C., & Dawson, K. (2010). The validation of one parental involvement measurement in virtual schooling. *Journal of Interactive Online Learning, 9*, 105–132.

Liu, F., & Cavanaugh, C. (2011). Success in online high school biology: Factors influencing student performance. *Quarterly Review of Distance Education, 12*, 37–54.

Lyons, J. F. (2004). Teaching U.S. history online: Problems and prospects. *The History Teacher, 37*, 447–456.

Mabrito, M. (2006). A study of synchronous versus asynchronous collaboration in an online business writing class. *American Journal of Distance Education, 20*, 93–107.

Maki, W., & Maki, R. (2002). Multimedia comprehension skill predicts differential outcomes in web-based and lecture courses. *Journal of Experimental Psychology, 8*, 85–98.

Maor, D. (2003). The teacher's role in developing interaction and reflection in an online learning community. *Educational Media International, 40*, 127–137.

McIsaac, M. S., Blocher, J. M., Mahes, V., & Vrasidas, C. (1999). Student and teacher perception of interaction in online computer-mediated communication. *Educational Media International, 36*, 121–131.

McLaughlin, J. A., & Lewis, R. B. (2004). *Assessing students with special needs* (6th ed.). Upper Saddle River, NJ: Prentice Hall.

McNeal, R. B. (2011). Labor market effects on dropping out of high school: Variation by gender, race, and employment status. *Youth & Society*, 305–332.

Menard-Warwick, J. (2009). Comparing protest movements in Chile and California: Interculturality in an Internet chat exchange. *Language and Intercultural Communication, 9*, 105–119.

Merryfield, M. M. (2003). Like a veil: Cross-cultural experiential learning online. *Contemporary Issues in Technology and Teacher Education, 3*, 146–171.

Michigan Merit Curriculum. (2006). *Online experience*. Retrieved from http://www.techplan.org/Online%20Experience%20Guidelines%202006.pdf

Moodle. (2012). Moodle myths. Retrieved from http://docs.moodle.org/23/en/Moodle_myths#With_Moodle.2C_you_need_to_be_on_computers_all_the_time

Moore, M. G. (2003). From Chautauqua to the virtual university: A century of distance education in the United States. Retrieved from ERIC database. (ED482357)

Moreno, R., & Mayer, R. E. (2002). Verbal redundancy in multimedia learning: When reading helps listening. *Journal of Educational Psychology, 94*, 156–163.

Murphy, E., Rodriguez-Manzanares, M. A., & Barbour, M. (2011). Asynchronous and synchronous online teaching: Perspectives of Canadian high school distance education teachers. *British Journal of Educational Technology, 42*, 583–591.

National Education Association. (2006). *Guide to teaching online courses*. Retrieved from http://www.nea.org/assets/docs/onlineteachguide.pdf

New Mexico Public Education Department. (2007). *SB209/HB201*. Retrieved from http://www.nmlegis.gov/lcs/legislation.aspx?Chamber=H&LegType=B&LegNo=201&year=07

Noble, D. F. (2001). *Digital diploma mills: The automation of higher education*. New York, NY: Monthly Review Press.

O'Dowd, R. (2003). Understanding the "other side": Intercultural learning in Spanish-English e-mail exchange. *Language Learning and Technology, 7*, 118–144.

Ormrod, J. E. (2008). *Educational psychology: Developing learners* (6th ed.). Upper Saddle River, NJ: Pearson.

Pape, L., Adams, R., & Ribeiro, C. (2005). The Virtual High School: Collaboration and online professional development. In Z. L. Berge & T. Clark (Eds.), *Virtual schools: Planning for success* (pp. 118–132). New York, NY: Teachers College Press.

Peterson, J. (2011, August 20). Social media law limits contact between teachers, students. *Springfield News-Leader*. Retrieved from http://www.news-leader.com/article/20110821/LIFE/108210327/Social-media-law-limits-contact-between-teachers-students?nclick_check=1

Picciano, A. G., & Seaman, J. (2009). *K–12 online learning: A 2008 follow-up of the survey of U.S. school district administrators*. Sloan Consortium. Retrieved from http://www.google.com/url?sa=t&rct=j&q=&esrc=s&source=web&cd=2&ved=0CEAQFjAB&url=http%3A%2F%2Fsloanconsortium.org%2Fpublications%2Fsurvey%2Fpdf%2Fk-12_online_learning_2008.pdf&ei=mNY8UMmTI8Xj0QGL54GQBw&usg=AFQjCNFW4ptiaqxYt4sFQ31Zd3UVELKvFw

Polly, D. (2013). Designing and teaching an online elementary mathematics methods course: Promises, barriers, and implications. In R. Hartshorne, T. L. Heafner, & T. M. Petty (Eds.), *Teacher education programs and online learning tools: Innovations in teacher preparation* (pp. 335–356). Hershey, PA: IGI Global.

Quinlan, A. M. (2011). 12 tips for the online teacher. *Phi Delta Kappan, 92*(4), 28–31.

Rice, K. L. (2006). A comprehensive look at distance education in the K–12 context. *Journal of Research on Technology in Education, 38*, 425–448.

Roblyer, M. D. (1999). Is choice important in distance learning? A study of student motives for taking Internet-based courses at the high school and community college levels. *Journal of Research on Computing in Education, 32*, 157–171.

Roblyer, M. D. (2006). Virtually successful: Defeating the dropout problem through online school programs. *Phi Delta Kappan, 88*(1), 31–36.

Roblyer, M. D., & Davis, L. (2008). Predicting success for virtual school students: Putting research-based models into practice. *Online Journal of Distance Learning Administration, 11*(4). Retrieved from http://www.westga.edu/~distance/ojdla/winter114/roblyer114.html

Roblyer, M. D., Davis, L., Mills, S. C., Marshall, J., & Pape, L. (2008). Toward practical procedures for predicting and promoting success in virtual school students. *American Journal of Distance Education, 22*, 90–109.

Roblyer, M. D., & Marshall, J. C. (2002). Predicting success of virtual high school students: Preliminary results from an educational success prediction instrument. *Journal of Research on Technology in Education, 35*, 241–255.

Rose, R. M., & Blomeyer, R. L. (2007). *North American Council for Online Learning research committee issues brief: Access and equity in online classes and virtual schools*. Retrieved from http://www.inacol.org/cms/wp-content/uploads/2012/11/iNACOL_AccessEquity_2007.pdf

Rovai, A. P. (2000a). Building and sustaining community in asynchronous learning networks. *Internet and Higher Education, 3*, 285–297.

Rovai, A. P. (2000b). Online and traditional assessments: What is the difference? *Internet and Higher Education, 3*, 141–151.

Rovai, A. P. (2001). Building classroom community at a distance: A case study. *Educational Technology Research and Development, 49*(4), 33–48.

Rovai, A. P. (2002). Sense of community, perceived cognitive learning, and persistence in asynchronous learning networks. *Internet and Higher Education, 5*, 319–332.

Rovai, A. P., & Gallien, L. B. (2005). Learning and sense of community: A comparative analysis of African American and Caucasian online graduate students. *Journal of Negro Education, 74*, 53–62.

Rovai, A. P., & Wighting, M. J. (2005). Feelings of alienation and community among higher education students in a virtual classroom. *Internet and Higher Education, 8*, 97–110.

Rumberger, R. W. (1987). High school dropouts: A review of issues and evidence. *Review of Educational Research, 57*, 101–121.

Servon, L. J., & Nelson, M. K. (2001). Community technology centers: Narrowing the digital divide in low-income, urban communities. *Journal of Urban Affairs, 23*, 279–290.

Shulman, L. S. (1987). Knowledge and teaching: Foundations of the new reform. *Harvard Educational Review, 57*, 1–22.

Skiba, R. J., & Peterson, R. L. (2003). Teaching the social curriculum: School discipline as instruction. *Preventing School Failure, 47*, 66–68.

Southern Regional Educational Board. (2006). *SREB essential principles of high-quality online teaching: Guidelines for evaluating K–12 online teachers*. Retrieved from http://info.sreb.org/programs/EdTech/pubs/PDF/Essential_Principles.pdf

Stearns, E., & Glennie, E. J. (2006). When and why dropouts leave high school. *Youth & Society, 38*, 29–57.

Tallent-Runnels, M. K., Thomas, J. A., Lan, W. Y., Cooper, S., Ahern, T. C., Shaw, S. M., & Liu, X. (2006). Teaching courses online: A review of the research. *Review of Educational Research, 76*, 93–135.

Tally, B. (2007). Digital technology and the end of social studies education. *Theory and Research in Social Education, 35*, 305–321.

Thomas, M. J. W. (2002). Learning within incoherent structures: The space of online discussion forums. *Journal of Computer Assisted Learning, 18*, 351–366.

Tomei, L. A. (2006). The impact of online teaching on faculty load: Computing the ideal class size for online courses. *Journal of Technology and Teacher Education, 14*, 531–541.

Tu, C. (2002). The relationship between social presence and online privacy. *Internet and Higher Education, 5*, 293–318.

Tu, C., & McIsaac, M. (2002). The relationship of social presence and interaction in online classes. *American Journal of Distance Education, 16*, 131–150.

Tunison, S., & Noonan, B. (2001). Online learning: Secondary students' first experience. *Canadian Journal of Education, 26*, 495–511.

VHS Collaborative. (2012). VHS member profile. Retrieved from http://thevhscollaborative.org/about-us/vhs-member-profile

Vygotsky, L. S. (1978). *Mind in society: The development of higher psychological processes*. M. Cole, V. John-Steiner, S. Scribner, & E. Souberman (Eds.). Cambridge, MA: Harvard University Press.

Wang, M., Sierra, C., & Folger, T. (2003). Building a dynamic online learning community among adult learners. *Educational Media International, 40*, 49–61.

Warschauer, M. (1998). Online learning in a sociocultural context. *Anthropology & Education Quarterly, 29*, 68–88.

Warschauer, M., & Matuchniak, T. (2010). New technology and digital worlds: Analyzing evidence of equity in access, use, and outcomes. *Review of Research in Education, 34*, 179–225.

Wasburn-Moses, L. (2011). An investigation of alternative schools in one state: Implications for students with disabilities. *Journal of Special Education, 44*, 247–255.

Waschull, S. (2005). Predicting success in online psychology courses: Self-discipline and motivation. *Teaching of Psychology, 32*, 190–192.

Watson, J., Murin, A., Vashaw, L., Gemin, B., & Rapp, C. (2011). *Keeping pace with K–12 online learning: An annual review of policy and practice*. Evergreen Education Group. Retrieved from http://kpk12.com/cms/wp-content/uploads/KeepingPace2011.pdf

Weiner, C. (2003). Key ingredients to online learning: Adolescent students study in cyberspace—the nature of the study. *International Journal on E-Learning, 2*, 44–50.

Whipp, J. L., & Chiarelli, S. (2004). Self-regulation in a web-based course: A case study. *Educational Technology Research and Development, 52*, 5–22.

Whittaker, C. R., Salend, S. J., & Duhaney, D. (2001). Creating instructional rubrics for inclusive classrooms. *Teaching Exceptional Children, 34*(2), 8–13.

Wiggins, G., & McTighe, J. (2005). *Understanding by design* (2nd ed.). Alexandria, VA: Association for Supervision and Curriculum Development.

Zucker, A., & Kozma, R. (2003). *The virtual high school: Teaching generation V.* New York, NY: Teachers College Press.

www.ingramcontent.com/pod-product-compliance
Lightning Source LLC
Chambersburg PA
CBHW021846220426
43663CB00005B/423